SEVEN CATS
AND THE
ART OF LIVING

SEVEN CATS
AND THE
ART OF LIVING

Written and Illustrated by

JO COUDERT

WARNER BOOKS

A Time Warner Company

Some of the names and identifications of people who appear in this book have been changed to protect their privacy.

Warner Books, Inc., 1271 Avenue of the Americas, New York, NY 10020

 A Time Warner Company

Printed in the United States of America
First Printing: October 1996
10 9 8 7 6 5 4 3 2 1

Library of Congress Cataloging-in-Publication Data

Coudert, Jo.
    Seven cats and the art of living / Jo Coudert.
        p. cm.
    ISBN 0-446-51961-8
    1. Cats—New Jersey—Biography. 2. Coudert, Jo. I. Title.
SF445.5.C655 1996
818'.5403—dc20

Book design and composition by Giorgetta Bell McRee

for
Connie Carey
and the cats

Contents

SEVEN CATS
AND THE
ART OF LIVING

The Beginning

The river is a good companion. Here, near its source, it is an amiable size and murmurs cheerfully as it makes its way around rocks. One hot and soft summer day, I sat on a terrace above the bank, following the slow turns of a leaf as it rode the current downstream and watching a robin splash through its bath in the shallows across the way where the water was the color of iced tea.

Bitty, one of the cats, came around the corner of the house. Concentrating furiously on the flight of a small white butterfly, he sank to a crouch. His tail twitched. He crept forward. He was totally in the moment, an absorption I envied, for I find it difficult to keep my footing on the narrow ledge of the present and frequently slip off into thoughts of the past or future. That day the sounds the river made were like laughter from a distant cocktail party and reminded me of the city where late I lived. The freshly bathed robin heading for a branch above my head drew my eyes upward and I saw beyond, in the flawless blue sky, a turkey vulture lazing on the air currents, leading me to reflect that if there is a future life and I am allowed a choice, I would be happy to accept the ugliness of the vulture in exchange for the free joy of surfing on the wind.

The cat jumped. The butterfly bounced out of reach, and Bitty, casting about for what he would do next, saw me. Calling out delightedly, he hastened across the lawn, leaped a border of pachysandra, and sprang into my lap. He stretched up to rub his head against my chin in greeting and answered my words to him with rumbling, throaty purrs that erupted into half-miaows. As my fingers rummaged in the tawny fur behind his ears, I counted again this cat's qualities. The youngest and newest of the cats, Bitty was an undistinguished tabby and not beautiful except as all cats in their neatness and grace are beautiful, but he lived at the exuberant edge of his capabilities. He was loving, intelligent, talkative, high-spirited, good-humored, zestful, gentle, and generous. He had, I told him teasingly, a fine talent for being a cat.

It occurred to me how good it would be to have a comparable talent for being a human being—for living fully, handling events equably, thriving on relationships. At that moment a comment read long

ago in an Ann Bridge novel came back to me:
"Truth, she thought, all the truths that anyone
could need to lead an admirable, a nearly perfect life,
lay spread out all round one all the time. . . " The
only requirement is that "one had got to annex
them, as it were, conquer them by force and make
them one's own, before one could use them." Did
this cat in my lap embody some of the truths that
are everywhere at hand and have only to be noticed
to become one's own?

I considered the possibility. Cats in general pos-
sess dignity and presence. They live at the center of
their own lives, not on the fringe of larger lives.
They do not abase themselves for love and acceptance. They have no gods, nor do they need them,
for they take responsibility for themselves. They
have individuality and a sense of their own worth.
Simplicity is theirs, composure, equanimity. They
make the best of the circumstances in which they
find themselves. They seem to have found a solution
to the problem, so knotty for human beings, of distance versus closeness, merging versus separateness—how to stay far enough away from others to be
one's own self, yet near enough to lessen one's alone-
ness. They appear, judging by their unique ability to
purr, to find a great deal of quiet satisfaction in life.
Add to this their legendary ability always to land on
their feet, and, yes, I could well imagine that something of worth about the art of living was to be
learned from cats.

If that was so, I did not lack for subjects, for at that time there were seven cats living at GoWell. Clearly, I am fond of cats and take pleasure in them, but I never intended to be surrounded by so many. I used to go on the theory that one cat would relate to me while two or more would relate more strongly to each other. I think now that I was wrong about this, but I acted on it for many years when I was traveling back and forth on weekends between a city apartment and this old house in the western hills of New Jersey. I had a golden retriever then, and it was quite enough to transport Hector, the dog, and Kate, the cat, and, often, one or more weekend guests in my little car.

A frequent weekend guest, Constance Carey, who had hitherto considered herself a dog person, was so impressed by Kate's strong personality that when she visited in Connecticut and observed a young barn cat huddled against a cellar door in zero-degree weather, she scooped it up and carried it back to New York with her. Thereafter, when Connie came to GoWell for the weekend, Pickles came along too.

On one such weekend a year later, Connie and I went to the movies in the neighboring town of Chester, and when we emerged into the chill midnight, we saw and heard a cat approach one couple after another as they headed for their cars, miaowing interrogatively as though hunting for his lost people. We were the last he came to. The parking lot was empty. All the stores were dark. The night was bitter. The cat, a long-haired, butterscotch-colored creature, spoke anxiously, urgently, to us when we leaned down to pet him. We picked him up and he did not struggle. We put him in the car and waited to see if he wished to get out. We started the car and waited again. He was uneasy but not unhappy and gave every indication that he considered us an acceptable port in his personal storm. On the way home, Connie, knowing that I did not want a second cat, remarked that if we could not locate his owner, she would not mind keeping this one because he seemed sweet and would undeniably be beautiful when cleaned up and well-fed. The next day we telephoned the police and the Humane Society and left both country and city phone numbers, but no one ever called about a lost butterscotch cat, so Connie had a second cat and the cat had a name—Chester, in honor of the place where he had been found.

The next time a cat in need of a home turned up, there was no one to take it but me. My resolution to stop at one was breached. Then it happened again. And again. Eventually, I found myself transporting four cats, plus dog, between city and country, a heavy-enough chore to have played a part in my decision to live permanently in the country.

One never thinks of oneself as a statistic, but when the demographers speak of the middle class moving out of the cities, I realize I count in that swelling percentage. I had always loved New York and never thought to leave it, but the city suddenly felt as though some critical mass had been reached, as though one person too many had joined the crowds in the streets and caused an explosion of elbows and incivility. One afternoon when my work was finished, I snapped the leash on Hector and headed for the Hudson River to enjoy the sunset. The West Side Highway was solid with cars. The air was not air but exhaust fumes. Horns sounded non-stop. I thought longingly of the green peace of the country. That weekend, when Sunday evening came around, instead of getting in the car, I went to bed at GoWell. And the next night, and the next.

I discovered I did not miss the city. I found I could work in the country. I nailed together a set of stairs to the second story of an old henhouse and fashioned a workspace for myself under the peaked roof. Now when I lifted my eyes from my writing table, I saw not brick walls but the tops of trees and sailing clouds, and when work was ended for the day, I walked out into the natural world, not into brokenness and harshness and rush. I stayed on through the summer, testing the solitude, on through the fall, into the winter, and when I realized I had made friends and a life in the country, the decision to live at GoWell was ratified.

A year later Connie ran into condominium difficulties in New York and I suggested she might like to try living in the country too. Pickles and Chester came to stay and for more than a year Connie commuted to the city, but finding life in the country as agreeable as I did, eventually she moved her psychotherapy practice to a nearby town and became another in the émigré statistics.

Because cats are wonderful companions but no good at long walks, after Hector died at fourteen, we picked out Freebie, a medium-sized, silky-haired, black, brown, and white dog, at the local animal shelter. Freebie came with a note from her previous owner saying she liked cats, and, indeed, that proved to be so, although the cats were not eager to test her liking and pretty much ignored the dog until Bitty came.

Bitty was the seventh cat. It is several years now since he set me to thinking about the only truly important question there is: How do you live a life? Other people go to sea or to the high Himalayas in search of answers, but I am not adventurous, so I have searched here, on the bank of the South Branch of the Raritan River, and it is to the cats I have looked, believing that it may be easier to observe in their simple behavior what works and what does not than to try to tease out conclusions from the more complex behavior of human beings. I am not absolutely sure that I agree with Carl Van Vechten's comment that "there is, indeed, no single quality of the cat that man could not emulate to his advantage." But I do think there is much to be learned from these wonderful creatures.

Bitty

Bitty appeared out of the blue. One Thanksgiving Day three guests and Connie and I decided on a walk after dinner even though the temperature was a stinging five degrees. We set out on the little road that runs past GoWell, humps over a defunct railroad crossing, and climbs, at first gradually, then steeply, out of the valley. Midway, a packed dirt road cuts across the face of the hills, and we turned into it, trying to catch our breath without drawing the crackling air too deeply into our lungs. Freebie, the dog, was in the lead. Suddenly, with loud, glad cries, a half-grown kitten shot from a clump of underbrush beside the road and raced to the dog. Freebie bristled and barked, but then, seduced by the obvious friendliness of the kitten, her plumed tail began to wave and she lowered her head to let the dancing kitten rub against her muzzle.

Having greeted the dog, the kitten hurried on to us, calling out his delight at finding himself no longer alone in the winter landscape. Connie picked the small creature up and tucked him into the front of her down jacket. Immediately he poked his head above the zipper and surveyed us all merrily. His eyes were shining, his coat was clean and smooth, and he appeared well-fed. It was apparent that he had not been on his own for long. We surmised that, as quick and small as he was, he had streaked out a momentarily opened door, perhaps when his owners were saying goodbye to Thanksgiving guests, and had run too far in his exuberance to find his way home again. We set about knocking on the doors of the few houses on the road. But no, no house had lost a kitten; no one recognized him.

"Good lord, now you've got seven cats," said Peter, one of our guests, as we turned away from the last possibility.

"Absolutely not," said Connie.

"Never," said I. "Six is enough. Six is too many. This one goes to the Humane Society tomorrow."

All the way down the mountain, as we chatted, the little cat with his button-bright eyes looked from one to another of us quite as though he were following our conversation, and whenever there was a pause, he himself spoke. His miaow was truncated, shorn of its first syllable, so that it came out as

"Wow," but "Wow" as a rock singer might deliver it: "Wow-ow," sometimes even "Wow-ow-ow!" The small cat clearly intended it to be his contribution to the conversation, and it led to the oddest impression of his being not a lone, lost creature but an articulate, self-possessed presence.

At home, we lined a basket with a bath towel and put the kitten in it on top of a chest in the kitchen. After a small snack of turkey, he obediently curled up and went to sleep. And slept through the departure of our guests and on into the evening. When later I went into the kitchen to make sandwiches, his head popped over the rim of the basket and we talked while I buttered the bread.

"Did you have a good sleep?" I asked. "Are you hungry? Would you like some more turkey?" To each of my comments, he replied, "Wow-ow," firmly, interrogatively, sympathetically, or fervently as he deemed appropriate. I was much amused and kept my side of the dialogue going to see how soon he would tire of it. But he did not, and if I fell silent while getting something from the refrigerator, upon my return to the counter he caught my eye and asked a clear question: "Wow-ow?"

"Goodness," I told him, "for such a little bit of a cat, you certainly are talkative."

He agreed enthusiastically: "Wow-ow!"

The resident cats began convening for supper, and the kitten scrambled out of the basket to greet them. Predictably, they reacted with outrage. Backs arched, tails swelled, and Trot, with a flat swipe of his paw, sent the newcomer sprawling. The kitten picked himself up, gave a shake to clear his head, and padded cheerfully forward again. This time Pickles fixed him with a baleful glare and growled. The kitten sank respectfully to the floor, but his equanimity was undisturbed, and as soon as Pickles relaxed, he came pleasantly forward. As it had been with Freebie, his unguarded friendliness was disarming. Sweet William moved over to make room for him, and he joined the line of cats at their supper bowls.

Often since then, when finding myself the outsider in a group, I have remembered that small scene. Hitherto, nailed to the floor in a corner by shyness and self-consciousness, I waited for someone to notice me, speak to me, make me welcome. But how much better it is, I have found, to take a leaf from Bitty's book, to go forward pleasantly, conveying good will, without waiting for signs of acceptance, showing interest in others without waiting for them to take an interest in me. The risk of rejections turns out to be not very great, no more than it was for Bitty. Yes, Trot took a swipe at Bitty and Pickles froze him with a glance, and, yes, I have been stared at frostily, have had a cold shoulder turned. It has given me pause, as it did Bitty, but the harm is undone a moment later when a more generous person smiles, speaks, and makes room for me in the circle.

For Bitty, his warmth, friendliness, and interest paid off handsomely. By the following morning, he had a name—Bitty, by default from "little bit of a cat"—and our plan to give him up to the problematic fate of an animal shelter had gone by the board. He had engaged our attention and almost immediately our affections because he had insisted on interacting with us. How captivating it is when a cat—or a person—likes to communicate, *wants* to communicate, insists on interacting, and how cold it is when the opposite is true.

In looks, brindle-coated Bitty was at best unprepossessing, at worst homely, but it is astonishing how looks cease to matter, or even be much noticed, when other appealing qualities are present. I once was introduced to an older woman on a hotel terrace in Bermuda and registered her as being one of the homeliest women I had ever seen, for she had sallow, sickly skin with circles under her eyes that were a bruised brown and sagged low on her cheeks, caused, I learned later, by a liver disease. Her looks were off-putting, but within moments I was smiling at something witty she had said and, drawn by her questions and comments, was chatting animatedly with her and beginning to like her quite a good deal. It is a figure of speech to say that you warm up to somebody, but it is quite true that you do begin to feel warm and good in the radiant presence of someone who is outgoing and interested.

• • •

In his first days with us, because he was still very young, Bitty slept a great deal, curling himself into the bottom of his basket on the chest in the kitchen. It was his place, his home base, and it was deliciously warmed by the winter sun slanting through a nearby window. In fact, such were its comforts that he was frequently joined, and eventually completely dispossessed, by one of the adult cats. This was Socksie, an amiable old gentleman who, after lean years of straydom, had insinuated his way into the house, taken early retirement, and eaten himself into stoutness. His rotundity gave him logistical problems in fitting under the basket handle while at the same time trying to curl into the basket, but purring loudly, perhaps to alert Bitty that he intended coming in, Socksie circled and scrunched until he had himself arranged with a minimum of overflow on the basket's sides. Just before the large cat's final subsidence, Bitty always managed to wiggle out from under and resettle himself in the curve of Socksie's body. Socksie then laid his uppermost paw over Bitty and the two of them settled into dozing in the shaft of sunlight.

But when there was activity in the house, Bitty was up and on hand, curious and involved. He quickly learned to pounce on demons under the blankets when I made a bed. He believed that soap bubbles popped for his delectation when I washed dishes and that I wielded a feather duster especially to allow him to practice his bird-pursuit skills. I, in

particular,
much more so
than Connie, was charmed
by Bitty's cheerfulness and communicativeness—she was more drawn to
Chester's reserve and Pickles's feistiness—so it was
that I spent a great deal of time with him, and Bitty
and I became close. If Connie picked him up, his
head swiveled to see where I was, and he scrambled
out of her arms and over tabletops to get to my lap.
When I left a room, he followed, his eyes alive with
curiosity as to where I was going and what I planned
to do.

Freebie was captivated by Bitty as completely as
I. She was understandably nervous the first several
times Bitty, hidden behind a chair, jumped and
tackled her hind leg, but she soon realized that it
was intended to be a game and invented a part for
herself that involved towing Bitty, clinging to her
hind leg, the length of the living room rug. She

enjoyed the game so much that if she came into the living room and found Bitty sleeping, she nosed him to wake him, turned around and presented her hind leg for Bitty to grab and be towed. If Bitty spurned the offer, she nosed him some more and rolled him over until Bitty began to wrestle her muzzle, and then Freebie shook her head back and forth and the game was on, a gentle wrestling match in which Bitty batted and boxed but never put out his claws and Freebie caught a leg or haunch in her mouth and shook it but never clamped down.

Part of the dog's affection for Bitty may have been gratitude. Although herself middle-aged, Freebie was rather new in the house, having come only a few months before Bitty. In those months she had tried patiently to make friends with the adult cats, assuming every posture of good will and nonaggressiveness she could muster to convince them that all she wished was their acceptance, but she had remained a rather lonely outsider, with Connie and me as her only friends.

She was especially devoted to Connie, who had been instrumental in her acquisition. Connie had seen her picture in a local paper that every week prints the photograph of a homeless cat or dog at the Humane Society in the hope that some reader will do just what Connie did: look at it and say, "That's the kind of pet I've always wanted." The staff at the Humane Society told us her history. She had belonged to a man who called her Sugar and lavished affection on her, but then the man had fallen in love with a lady and no longer had time for Sugar, who resented her neglect and took it out in fierce jealousy of the fiancée. This cost Sugar her happy home. The young man had her professionally bathed, brushed, trimmed, and bedecked with a yellow ribbon so that she would be as presentable as possible for adoption and then drove her to the Humane Society and left her.

When Connie and I went to meet Sugar, we passed through a door into the pen area, setting off ear-splitting pleas for attention from all the dogs there. Except Sugar. She was sitting, small and still, in the exact center of the concrete floor of a wire mesh run. I stopped to pet a golden retriever and watched while Connie approached the cage. Sugar looked at her expressionlessly. The dog seemed in shock, as though the wrench away from everything familiar had been so extreme that there was no way to survive it except by keeping perfectly still, as a person who has been hurt will lie motionless for fear of setting off spasms of pain. Thirty other dogs barked and leaped and stood on their hind legs trying to thrust their noses through the chain link cages to gain our attention, but Sugar simply looked back at Connie.

I left off petting the retriever and joined Connie in front of the cage. My liking is for large dogs with square muzzles and luxuriant fur, and had the choice been solely mine, I would have taken the retriever, but I agreed that this dog about the size of a border collie was pretty and that it was probably just as well, with all the cats, not to take a dog as large as the retriever. As we talked, looking at her, a light began to come into Sugar's eyes, and very slowly, very tentatively she wagged the tip of her tail. Just the tip. Just once.

Connie crouched down. "Come here," she said. "Come and see if you like us." With more coaxing, Sugar approached to sniff at Connie's hand. The tip of her tail wagged once more. "Yes, she's the right dog," Connie said.

And so we took Sugar home. Neither of us liked her name. While casting about for a new one, we were hearing the cry of a flycatcher who was nesting on top of a pillar on the porch and frequently sat on a telephone wire out front, calling, "Phoebe! Phoebe!" Connie decided the name Phoebe suited our timid soul. The next day, with a slip of the tongue, it became Freebie, and since she had indeed been a freebie, that is what it remained.

At first, Freebie was agonizingly afraid of being in the wrong or in the way and cowered and clung to the edges of rooms and hid if anyone came to the door. But one day, taken unawares, she surprised herself by barking furiously at a stranger, and that seemed to convince her that it was her house to protect and we were her people to relate to. Happiness seeped back into her being. On her walks with

Connie, she began to step out briskly, head high, feathery tail, which had mostly been tucked between her legs, now tracing delicate arcs over her back. There was a residual timidity and anxiousness to please, but that was perhaps basic to her nature. Her only sorrow in her new life, as far as we could discern, was that the cats, although they understood that she was not to be feared, could not be persuaded that she was to be loved and allowed to play with them and sleep with them. Time and again, Freebie proposed to join them, and time and again they moved away and left her looking wistful.

But Bitty remedied that, and Freebie's world became complete. She loved the little kitten— watched over him, swept her tail back and forth across the floor for Bitty to play with, and remained painstakingly quiet when Bitty pillowed his head against her and slept. Are there affinities between animals as there are between people? I believe there must be, and between animal and person as well. A woman who already had seven cats and four dachshunds once explained to me that she had bought a Himalayan cat she certainly did not need and could ill afford because their eyes had locked through a pet shop window and, she said, "I knew we could have a special relationship." She was a silly woman, but I think in this she was aware of a truth. Bitty and Freebie had a special relationship, as did Bitty and I.

• • •

Apart from everything else, I was ravished by Bitty's cheerfulness. I did not realize that I had come to value cheerfulness quite so much until a time when I went to a chiropractor for that most common of complaints: an aching back. On a Monday after a particularly rainy weekend, as the fellow rotated his thumbs on my sciatic nerves, he commented on the weather and then added with a deep sigh, "Ah, but the weather doesn't matter when you're in love." I made such conventional noises of agreement and approval as I could muster facedown, but what sprang to mind was, "Love's all very well, my friend, but don't marry the girl unless she's cheerful."

Perhaps cheerfulness is immoderately important to me because I lived for long periods of my life with people whose prevailing filter was gray, who moved without lightness, greeted the day with no particular joy, and did not remark the delight to be found in small things. If an excursion was planned, the talk was not of the pleasant destination but of the likelihood of getting caught in a traffic jam on the way. If the decision was to stay home to avoid the traffic, that was just as gloomy a prospect because that meant being faced with all the mundane chores that needed doing. Life, to such people, was a repeated opportunity for things to turn out badly.

These were not clinically depressed people; they were attractive, competent, and well-functioning, and in their pessimism they were no different from the majority of people, for more people than not have this mildly depressive set toward life. It is a cheerful outlook that is uncommon. I once over-heard a psychoanalyst comment wistfully that he envied people who were born hypomanic, that is, just manic enough to be characteristically good-humored and upbeat. I was young enough then to scorn his remark because I thought that pessimism was profound and cheerfulness shallow, that somber-ness indicated a serious and sophisticated nature while sunniness suggested a failure to appreciate the point of life. I cannot remember when I began to realize this was nonsense. Perhaps it dawned on me gradually as I saw how lives were drained of color and interest and spirit by pessimism and how sel-dom the constantly predicted difficulties came to pass, or if they did eventuate, how easily they could be dealt with.

People who take a dim view of things claim they are being realistic, not pessimistic. But you can pre-dict accurately and still not have the pessimism be realistically justified. You can, for instance, predict the traffic jam and not only be right but have the prediction come true in spades, as it did one broil-ing summer day for two of us on the Long Island Expressway. It was a Friday afternoon and we were on our way to spend the weekend with friends. The stream of cars, always close to solid on this arterial highway, slowed abruptly and stopped dead. We learned later that ahead of us a truck carrying cases of mayonnaise had overturned, greasing the road and causing any number of cars to slide into each other. Trapped there for four hours, did we become hysterical, angry, despairing? None of these things. We played word games. We sang. We opened the packages intended to be our contribution to the weekend and picnicked on Stilton, sausage, French bread, grapes, and strawberries. Such times are terrible in prospect, but when they actually do happen, you play it as it lays.

Getting stuck in a traffic tie-up is a small thing. But life is chiefly made up of small things, and how they are anticipated and how they are handled go a long way in determining whether daily life is an enjoyable affair or a dreary slog or even actively awful. In addition, how people view small mishaps is suggestive of how they will manage large misfortunes. People who are cheerful tend to find ways out of crises. The disaster does not go so deep nor last so long as it does for the person who believes that now that this unfortunate thing has happened, this too will probably go wrong, and this, and this, which very well might be true since to take a gloomy view is the most certain way of bringing further troubles on.

I have sometimes wondered if Bitty was dumped by the side of the road that Thanksgiving Day. It seems unthinkable that anyone would be so cruel to a bright and loving creature, but let us assume that Bitty was unwanted and discarded. Had he been a cat who took a dim view of things, he might not have emerged from the thicket when we passed by because he would have had no faith in the kindness of strangers. Instead, he would have cowered there and died of exposure. Or if he had made his presence known to us but had acted dull and depressed, he would have been packed off to the Humane Society the next day, confirming his belief that the world was a malign place and he was right to be pessimistic. But Bitty was cheerful, and, as I say, a cheerful disposition tends to bring about happy endings.

Happy yourself, you are a source of happiness to others, which makes you well-liked, and this in turn redounds to increase your pleasure in life, ensuring that it will be far from the mundane and somewhat burdensome affair it is to so many people.

I have a friend, made since I moved to the country, who is ninety years old. After her car had a brush with the wing mirror of a truck a year ago, her driver's license was revoked and she was, as she puts it, "grounded." Since she lives on eighty acres and the lane to her house is long and twisting, that unfortunate happening would seem to have presaged the end of her social life. On the contrary, friends—all of them one, two, even three generations younger—never feel it is too much trouble to pick her up, whether it is for a shopping expedition, a garden tour, or no more than a visit over a glass of iced tea. I myself collect Alice when I have errands to do because she is marvelous company, always cheerful and always interested even if we are doing nothing more intriguing than rummaging around in a hardware store or looking at fabrics or going through wallpaper books. She comments, she reacts, she asks questions and takes delight in colors, shapes, and textures. We chat nonstop and the talk is punctuated with laughter. Alice's cheerfulness guarantees that even at ninety she has a life filled with friends and companionship, a great contrast to the complaint of most old people that they are abandoned to loneliness and isolation.

Should I add here that my ninety-year-old friend's health is excellent? It is unquestionably hard to be cheerful when you do not feel well. But when considering health and cheerfulness, it is difficult to say which is cause and which effect, for more and more research indicates that a cheerful and optimistic approach to life goes a long way toward bolstering one's immune system and preserving health. It is no accident that a woman who reacts with unshakable depression to being abandoned by her husband, as one of my old acquaintances did, is found to have pancreatic cancer two years later. We all get cancer all the time, in that aberrant or defective cells are a common occurrence, but the body's defenses simply surround such cells and hustle them off before they can reproduce themselves and establish a colony. In the presence of depression, however, it is not merely the spirits that are depressed but the immune system as well. Just as a depressed person does not perform his work effectively, so also does the immune system lie down on the job, allowing things to begin to go wrong.

Bitty, when he rushed out of the thicket and hurried to us, was not in search of happiness. He was looking for food and shelter and company. That he found happiness with us was because he brought it with him.

A great deal of Bitty's pleasure in life came, I think, from his taking an intense interest in the world around him. While it is perfectly true that a cat has nothing better to do, it occurs to me that neither has a person. We have worse things to think about, of course, such as our own problems, and that is what our minds return to again and again unless, as novelist Edith Wharton recommended, we take hold of life as it lies around us. The world is profoundly interesting. People are engaging. To find them so, the only requirement is that we be alert and responsive, that we think about what we are seeing and hearing, think beyond ourselves, outside of ourselves.

There is someone close to me who comes to visit bursting with troubles. I take her on a walk on a country road, and when I say, "Look, there are wild ducks on the pond," she glances and says, "Yes, isn't that nice," and returns instantly to studying my face as she recounts the difficulties of her life. At the end of the day, I sense how let down she is as she drives away because I have been unable to lighten her troubles. The ducks might have. If she had truly seen them, if she had seen the world as we walked, she would have moved out of the personal and found some relief from the swarming problems chattering in her brain.

Obsession with the personal ravages our lives. When we can see only our own problems, we have very little perspective and no distance, which makes the problems seem huge. But when we take our place in the world, we have the perspective of being part of something much larger that has a natural rhythm of growth and decay; we understand that we are a link in a chain of life that recedes immeasurably behind us and stretches infinitely ahead of us. Being aware of that, we come to appreciate the double truth that while our individual problems matter greatly, they really do not matter very much at all.

In February, the weather, which had been despotic, began to loosen its grip and let occasional hours slip through when it was possible to work outside. February work in a garden is slight; the only major task at GoWell is pruning the grapevine, disentangling the long whips and snipping them back to just two buds each. Bitty was, at first, diverted by the pile of stalks on the ground, treating them as snakes to be combatted, but when he could no longer persuade himself they were alive, he moved on to a loose rock wall and scrabbled over it, pick-

ing up the scent of a chipmunk and peering into
crevices for the sight of one. I kept an eye on him
while I pruned, but when he was immobile, I could
not pick him out against the background of stones
and had to call his name and wait for his answering,
"Wow-ow." It was then that I began to understand
why tabby cats are so common. The tawny striped
coat has great utilitarian value as camouflage against
rocks, tree trunks, leaves, and dried grasses.

Another February garden task was to pick up
sticks. Nature is a grand pruner; snow, wind, and
rain bring down twigs, branches, and limbs, briskly
weeding out the infirm, diseased, and dead.
Gathering the debris was no particular fun, and in
deference to my back I did not do much of it at a
time. Instead, when I had an armload, I called to
Bitty and walked back along the river into the
woods to add the sticks to the brush pile there.

The woods quickly became Bitty's favorite place.
He raced through the fallen leaves, let his momen-
tum carry him six feet up the trunk of a tree,
dropped down again, sprang from rock to rock along
the riverbank, and peered and sniffed down holes.
Taking a cue from his interested inspection of everything in his path, I tried to substitute true seeing for
general impressions. It has been said that to truly
see, it is necessary to forget the name of what you are
looking at, so I made myself not say "river" when I
looked at the water. Instead, I leaned against a tree
and *looked*—at a silver sheet where the surface was

unbroken, at the crackling sparkles in the stony shallows, at the reflections that broke and came together again, at the twig that had fallen on the river's surface and was now being lightly borne to the sea or, more likely, to one of the bends downstream where it would become part of a growing dam nudging the river to remake itself.

As well as trying to see without naming, I tried to hear without identifying the sounds. Two things were startling: how silent it was, and how noisy. At first, I was conscious of the stillness, then I became conscious of the noise, not just woods noise of creaking limbs and rustling leaves but people noise. I once heard a sound engineer describe how, wanting to make a recording in an environment absolutely free of human sounds, he had journeyed into remote forests, only to find that no matter how far he was from civilization, there was always the drone of an airplane or the far-off scream of a chainsaw. That was, of course, doubly and triply true in my patch of woods. I felt isolated, but as I paid attention to what I was hearing, I picked up a steady hum from cars on the road a mile away and, from the sky, distant jet engines.

I was listening one day, expecting to pick up only these background noises and, in the foreground, the dropping of a nut from a tree or the plunk of a pebble dislodged by Bitty, when there came the sound of something else, something large and stealthy moving in the brush across the river—one step, a

wait, one step, a wait. Bitty heard it too and flat-
tened himself into a bump on a log. We each stared
tensely as the tangled thicket directly across the
river stirred and rustled. Branches swayed. Twigs
snapped. The brush parted just enough for a head to
come through, and there across the river, a deer
peered out. She was a large doe with eyes as deep and
shiny as pools of oil and ears that continually made
fine directional adjustments to monitor every quar-
ter of her environment. She was gazing directly
across at me, but as long as I was motionless, she
apparently did not identify the shape she was seeing
as human.

But I did move. A bug flew in my face and involuntarily I lifted my hand to brush it away. The deer
was there and then she was not there. Like the
Cheshire cat, she vanished and only the gentle peering of her eyes remained behind. Bitty looked up at
me. "Yes, Bitty," I said, "that was exciting, wasn't it,
to see a deer like that." Bitty shook himself as
though coming out of a dream.

On another day a woodchuck came ambling down
the path toward us with the air of a sweet, somewhat
addled old lady bumbling along. Bitty hid behind a
tree and watched her, then bounced up and danced
down the path to meet her. When the chuck realized
the cat was there, she reared up and settled solidly
on her haunches, her short front paws folded sedate-
ly on her breast, and studied the cat nearsightedly.
Bitty crouched down and inched closer and closer.

The woodchuck, looking as benign as the Pope, raised one front paw, probably in warning but seemingly in benediction, and sat there blessing Bitty as Bitty crawled forward, stretching as close as he could while nevertheless braced to spring backward, and sniffed. He sniffed and sniffed, rolling the scent around his nasal passages until he reached an understanding of what the woodchuck was all about. Then he withdrew, backing off slowly, and the woodchuck dropped to all fours and continued on her solemn way.

In the world of nature, there are such moments, moments of deep pleasure so absent of self that they approach ecstasy or enlightenment. Bitty showed me a way to be undeceivably alive by being in the world instead of walking through it, by seeing rather than looking, listening rather than hearing.

As spring advanced, unlocking the earth, the work of the garden was on me in a rush. One day it was too early to rake the leaves off the flower beds. A day later I was fearful I had waited too long. Daffodils speared through dead leaves and wore them like ruffs. Tulip stalks bent under the weight of the mulch. Now every afternoon was spent raking and carting, cleaning and tilling. No time now to spend in simplicity with Bitty, but still we stayed in relation. I had the sense that he always knew where I was even after he grew tired of following me back and forth as I hauled debris to the compost pile, and I, when I grew conscious of not glimpsing his small body in some time, called his name and listened for his acknowledging "Wow-ow." If he heard me, he answered, but he was growing up and was often engaged in fearless adventuring beyond the sound of my voice.

Soon he was following the senior cats across the road to hunt the fields there. The fields, previously used to grow corn, had not been planted in several years and were rapidly springing up in dense growth. The cats spent hours prowling the paths through the brush and tall weeds, moving in a miniature kingdom of their own. It was strange to realize how divided their life was between the civilized house and the wild fields. When Bitty had been missing too long and I crossed the road to look for him, I could sense how exciting the contrast must be. In many places the raspberry and rose canes, the bristling thistle plants, the whips of sumac grew too thickly for me to make my way through. When I knelt to peer down tunneled rabbit paths, it was easy to imagine how much like lions the cats must feel, stalking this jungle. More than any other animal, a cat can live in two worlds—and move, seemingly without a sense of dislocation or incongruity, between them. In this world of the field, the cats stalked game—mice, moles, voles, rats, chipmunks, and rabbits; then they crossed the road and lay in laps and ate their food from china dishes.

I was not happy about Bitty, or any of the cats, crossing the road because, although traffic on the road was light, the cars came from three directions: down the mountain, along the river, or over the bridge. The road converged in a Y in front of the house and the cats crossed at the widest point. But the fields, night and day, were irresistible to them, and the only way to keep them safe would have been to keep them inside. I know people who do that, even in the country—label the cat a house cat and never allow it outside. But I do not believe in safety, not at the cost of freedom. Life is free, varied, exciting, and provocative, or it is nothing.

Several years ago I frightened myself by buying a little blue motor scooter. I felt that it was completely likely that I might be killed on the narrow, twisting, cambered country roads around GoWell, but somehow I knew it was right to get the scooter, that if I drew back in fear, my life would begin to narrow and my spirit to wither. I still heave a sigh of relief each time I arrive back home in one piece after a cruise on the scooter, but at the same time the scooter has given me immense amounts of pleasure and an incomparable delight in my own daring. Which is why the cats stay free: it is better that they risk the road and live every bit of life they can lay hold of than stay home in safety and live only a little.

When I went river rafting, the tables were turned and it was Bitty who worried about me. The river, which melds with two others many miles south of here and becomes huge by the time it reaches Perth Amboy and the ocean, at my stretch of it is essentially a trout stream, knee-deep, with a rocky bottom, an occasional pool, and miniature rapids above and below the bridge near the house. It is not deep enough to swim in so I sit on an air mattress and push upstream with my sneakered feet and then float back down and shoot the rapids.

On the first really hot day of summer, I started out to do just this. I had gone only a few yards upstream when I heard anxious, urgent cries. Bitty slid down the bank to the water's edge, jumped to a rock in the stream, and strained toward me just short of the point at which he must fall in. He warned me with all the urgency he could pack into his cries that I was in severe danger and should set about saving myself immediately. When, instead, I continued recklessly to push upstream, he followed, leaping from rock to rock, sometimes getting wet to his shoulders, all the time calling out his concern. I kept telling him that it was all right, but he would not be reassured.

Above the bend in the river I braced my feet against a boulder and sat for a time, enjoying the contrast of cool water on my legs and warm sun on my back. Bitty paced at the river's edge, still talking to me about his worries. Thinking to show him there was nothing to fear, I drifted over to the bank, picked him up, put him in my lap, and pushed off into the current. The little cat went utterly still. He jammed his back against me and stared down at the water. He made not a sound, moved not a muscle. Thus we rafted silently downriver. I assumed he was revising his opinion of the river, coming to understand its friendly dimension. Not a bit of it. The current, when we neared the house, brought us within six feet of the bank. Suddenly, without shifting, without tensing a muscle, without a hint to me, Bitty launched himself, arcing through the air in a great leap. He had calculated to a nicety: his back feet landed at the very edge of the water. He was up the bank in three bounds, where he turned, fixed his eyes on me, and resumed his hectoring about the danger I was in.

So it went through the summer. Whenever I rafted on the river, Bitty followed along the bank crying his alarm. To love is to give hostages to fate. Bitty agonized over my safety, but would that have been reason enough for him to refuse to love? Many people think that way: that one should protect oneself against hurt by not getting too deeply attached. Bitty would have dismissed such a notion. Love unreservedly, love uncritically, love openly, warmly, delightedly, is what I learned from Bitty, and deal with the loss when it comes.

I cannot deny that it is far easier to care uncomplicatedly about an animal than a person. How can I deny it when I can see in my own life how love of a person has often been mixed with need and need has made me peevish and cautious? That is one reason I was grateful to Bitty: he let me experience the free delight of loving unconditionally; he let me learn that I am capable of it. I wish it had been a person I loved with all my heart, but if that cannot be, at least I have known what it is to care utterly for a creature that is not myself.

I wonder if that is why we have pets?

Poppy

One Saturday morning long before Bitty came, at a time when Kate was my only cat, I became aware of quarrelsome voices on the bridge. Curious, I stepped out on the porch and spotted three children from up the road standing near the rail. The eldest, a girl, kept revolving to shield something clutched to her chest from the grasping hands of her brothers. "No," she insisted over their clamor. "No, no, no."

"What's up?" I asked, strolling to join them.

Sally had tears of upset in her eyes. "Joey and Jeff want to throw the cat in the river," she said, "and I say we should put her in the woods." She opened her arms to show me a black and gray striped cat she had in a stranglehold. The struggling cat's fur stood on end in every direction and her eyes blazed with fear. I recognized her as one of a litter of six the children had invited me to come see some months before, hoping I would adopt one or more of them, which I had declined to do on the basis that it would upset my Persian, who did not like her turf invaded. This was true enough, but even so, I would not have taken one of the kittens because, tossed, teased, and terrorized by the children, they were nerve-ridden, so reactive that they flew into the air, stiff-legged, at every sound, made wild, aimless dashes up and over chair backs, and attacked any hand reaching out to stroke them.

The children said that they had managed to find homes for five of the six kittens but no one wanted this last one. After two reprieves, their father had this morning announced that the cat went today— or else. The "or else" was unspecified, but I gathered the threat was delivered in enough of a roar to send the children scurrying down the road with the creature. Their intent was to abandon her to fate when they got far enough away from the house, whether fate took the form of her living wild in the woods or finding refuge in a barn or being dispatched by a speeding car. But when they came to the bridge, it occurred to the boys that it would be more interesting to drop the cat in the river. If the creature could swim, she could start her odyssey when she reached the bank. If she couldn't . . . Either way, they would have gotten rid of her, as their father ordered.

Cats can swim if they have to, and I did not want

the creature. Why, then, did I pick her out of Sally's viselike grip and carry her into the house? I suppose I saw myself in the role of rescuer to the sorely tried animal. This is very like the trap a person—most often a woman—walks into when she decides to rescue a fellow human being from failure, unhappiness, or addiction. She can be open-eyed about the other's problems, as I was about Poppy's, but she is misty-eyed about her own sense of how good she is going to be for this damaged other, how *remedial*. Her forbearance, her tenderness, her patience will repair the damage done by the insensitive world and rescue the person from his self-defeating ways—or so she tells herself. And so I told myself about the striped cat.

Because an endearing name makes an animal more appealing, I called the cat Poppet, which eased into Poppy, and I set about being wonderful to her. I spoke softly, was careful about moving abruptly or unexpectedly, stroked her gently, never teased her, and did not attempt to play with her for fear she would interpret it as aggression. Even so, as the weeks went by, Poppy continued to cower if I looked at her, flee if I went toward her, and struggle and cry if I picked her up. Nothing persuaded her that the present was different from the past or that life was any better for her than it had ever been.

Years before, out of a passing curiosity, I had undertaken an experiment to test whether the experiences of infancy are indeed as formative as Freudian theory has it. It was when I had just recently acquired the house in the country. Friends were visiting for the weekend and they thought they might like to do what I was doing, that is, find a wreck of a place, buy it for very little, and fix it up, so I took them up the mountain to look at an old tenant farmer's house that was standing empty and open to the elements. When we stepped over the threshold, a pile of rags in the corner moved and Christine and I backed away, fearing it was a nest of rats or mice. But Joe was braver and went forward to discover that the blind blobs crawling there were kittens a few days old. Now that I think back, it seems obvious that the mother cat fled when she heard us coming, but at the time we assumed the kittens were abandoned and we scooped them up and carried them back to the house.

When it appeared that efforts to keep the kittens alive were going to succeed, it occurred to me to wonder whether differences in the way they were being treated would have a perceptible effect on their personalities. Peaches, the prettiest one, from the start had been fed first, handled the most, and fussed over, while the unattractive runt of the litter was fed last and given almost no attention. The runt was a scrawny, all-black kitten with dull, lifeless fur, a sharp face, and ears at such a funny angle that he was referred to as Bat Cat. In the sleeping heap of kittens he was the one on the bottom, the one the others stepped on, climbed over and pushed aside, the clumsy one. When the kittens were handled, he was seldom picked up, petted, or spoken to. I thought it might be interesting to see whether changing all that would bring about any change in him.

First came a new name: Boston—because he was black and there was a radio character known as Boston Blackie. Then a different feeding order; the runt was fed first instead of last and given a second bottle and a third until he was blissfully full, and all the time he ate I held him close and spoke his name, telling him what a fine and special fellow he was. During the day while I was working at my desk, I tucked him into the front of my sweater and he slept against my beating heart as he had slept against his mother's, and when I took a break from work, I cradled him in my hands so he could see my face and again talked to him softly and affectionately.

Within a day Boston's head turned to follow the sound of my voice. Another day and he no longer accepted to be on the bottom of the kitten heap but struggled out from under and worked his way to the top. He was the first of the kittens to open his eyes, the first to purr and make clumsy efforts to wash himself, the first to struggle over the side of the box and set out on wobbly legs to explore the world. But the most surprising thing was how his looks changed. It was like watching the tide go out and leave the sand shining. The fur on his face took on the sheen of silk, then day by day the sheen moved down his body until he gleamed like a jet bead from the tip of his little black nose to the tip of his tail.

It seemed reasonable to assume that it might be somewhat encouraging to an infant to be cherished, but I had not guessed that it would be transforming. It was as though, by giving Boston love and attention, I had given him permission to like and value himself. Feeling secure allowed him to become adventurous and outgoing. Feeling loved, he loved everybody and took it for granted he was loved equally in return. His intelligence flowered, and he developed an extraordinary vocabulary. Bitty, who came long after Boston was gone, talked a great deal but his "words" were all variations on one sound, whereas Boston could make about forty different sounds, each with a specific meaning.

The picture Boston gained in those early weeks of life of the world as a benevolent and rewarding place, of people as nurturing and gratifying, of himself as a valued, competent, and worthwhile creature became the matrix of his personality and he lived a sunny, loving, and much-loved life because of it, a life quite the opposite of Poppy's.

Like Poppy and Boston, any creature newly arrived in the world, whether animal or human, sets about developing a picture of what the world is like. It is as though there are pieces of a puzzle scattered about and it is the infant's task to fit them together as quickly as possible to get an idea of what he will be dealing with in this place in which he finds himself. The pieces Poppy was provided were the opposite of the ones that came Boston's way. Poppy's infancy, dominated by three young children in a noisy household, gave her a picture of the world as confusing and unpredictable, of herself as an object to be pounced on, thrown in the air, hugged tight or forgotten, put in a warm box or left to cry unheeded in the cold.

Instead of developing a basic trust toward the world as Boston did, Poppy developed a basic fear of it. To deal with her anxiety, she could have become oversubmissive and self-effacing, trying to win tolerance and acceptance by being no trouble to anyone; or she could have become overaggressive and truculent, fighting back against the injustices done her; or she could have withdrawn from contact as much as possible, trying to become self-sufficient and independent. Poppy chose to withdraw. As soon as I set her down in the house that Saturday morning, she fled to the cellar, jumped on top of the washing machine and from there to a pipe in the ceiling where she worked some insulation loose and crawled into a black hole between the rafters.

Ever after that when we were at GoWell, Poppy spent the major part of her days in that black hole. If the door to the cellar was closed, she lay on her side and clawed at it, and when I came by, she pleaded with frantic miaows for me to open it. If I ignored her, she became so desperate that I had to relent. Even after Socksie and Trot came and she allowed herself to care for them, that black hole was essentially where Poppy lived her life.

I bore not the slightest resemblance to three hyperactive children. But Poppy saw those children when she saw me. To her, all the world remained as she had pieced her picture of it together originally. Seeing this I begin to understand why it is so difficult for one person to change another. In the past I have sometimes assumed that all I had to be was accepting and supportive enough, understanding and patient enough, and it would surely short-circuit the self-defeating behavior of the person I cared about. But however hard I tried, my behavior, even if it seemed to be just about all anyone could ask for, never made any lasting difference. I realized with Poppy that it could not. What mattered was not what I did but how the other viewed the world. That is what had to change if the other was to change.

Alas, as Poppy demonstrated, it is very difficult to

alter those first impressions, to rearrange the puzzle pieces to come up with a different picture. Perhaps this is understandable if one pictures the newborn brain to be like a road after a heavy snowfall. The first car down it establishes parallel ruts, and the next car tends to follow in those ruts, and the next and the next. The ruts get dug deeper and deeper, and however much the hundredth car might intend to take a different route, it soon slips into the established way.

Perceptions following in the ruts of the earliest ones laid down etch the pathways in the psyche deeper and deeper, and the hundredth observation is no more likely than the hundredth car to be successful at taking a new route. Something learned about people or the world yesterday can be readily revised or abandoned on the basis of contrary evidence, but beliefs etched early in life remain in force in the face of the most convincing evidence to the contrary. Poppy was proof of that, for there was no behavior of mine, however innocuous, however tender, however undirected at her, that did not slip directly into the rut of threat, to be interpreted by her as an intention to harm or harass her.

An infant's field of experience is extremely limited, his contact with people is confined to just a few. He cannot weigh and judge and compare; he has to work with what comes within his ken. Cat or person, if he is lucky in his handling, like Boston, the pathways laid down will be that the world is a

benevolent place where his efforts will be applauded, his wishes gratified, his security assured. He will
think well of himself and, expecting to be loved, he
will go out in love. Unlucky, like Poppy, and he will
believe that the world is an inimical place, that people are not to be looked to for succor or satisfaction,
that he will never be happy, and that for some reason that eludes him but must somehow have to do
with his own unworthiness, he does not deserve a
better fate.

Boston and Poppy were both perfectly right in
the way they saw the world. But not because of the
way the world is; because of the way they were. They
brought on themselves the experiences that confirmed their beliefs. Boston was loved because he
was loving. Poppy had a terrible life because she
believed life was terrible.

Poppy had been with me about a year when she
developed an abscess over one eye, worrisome in
both location and depth, and hours after it had been
opened and drained and I had brought her back
home, she went into shock, turning limp and cold.
I bundled her into the car and rushed her, on telephoned instructions, not to the vet's office, which
was closed for the weekend, but to the vet's house,
where I had to leave her because I was due back in
the city for a meeting. When I called the next
evening to check on how Poppy was doing, I
received assurances so vague as to be baffling. The

following evening our conversation was equally abstract: the vet *thought* the abscess was clearing, she *thought* Poppy was probably going to be all right but she really could not be sure and she did not want me to be too optimistic . . .

On the third night, I said, "Poppy's gone, isn't she?"

"No, no, she's alive."

"I mean, she's disappeared. You can't find her."

"Oh, dear . . ."

Sensing that the vet was on the verge of tears, I said hastily, "It's okay. She's in a hole somewhere. I know Poppy."

"I've looked everywhere. I've torn the house apart. I've asked my husband for a divorce."

"What!"

It turned out that the vet had put Poppy in a guest bathroom at the end of the upstairs hall, with strict instructions to her husband not to go in it on any account, instructions he forgot when he, a large-animal veterinarian, was called out in the middle of the night to treat a mare in trouble delivering a foal. Husband and wife had had a terrible fight, she blaming him for letting the cat escape, he blaming her for blaming him when all he had been trying to do was not to wake her by using the bathroom at the end of the hall.

"We haven't spoken since," the vet finished her story. "Not one word. I don't know what's going to happen."

"I do," I said. "I'll bring Hector. He'll find Poppy."
And that is what happened. Golden retrievers had
bloodhound in their original breeding and they have
terrific noses. Hector knew Poppy's name and, told
to find her, he ranged through the house eagerly,
sniffing, backtracking, sniffing again, and finally set-
tling on the bathroom and a floor-to-ceiling cupboard built in at one end of the bathtub.

"But I've looked there a dozen times," the vet
protested. Hector wagged his tail enthusiastically,
and when she opened the cupboard to show him it
was bare of cat, he inched his way to a back corner
and barked. Sure enough, there was a hole in the par-
tition next to the tub. Trust Poppy to find a black
hole. But even a scared cat has to eat and we lured her
out with the smell of food, saving the vet's marriage.

Poppy defined the vet's pleasant home as a
slaughterhouse, and in light of that she did the reasonable thing, secreting herself where she could not
be found and destroyed. Of course, she put herself in
danger of starving to death. But that is not surprising. Cats—and people—often do things severely
against their own best interests because they are
thinking along ancient lines.

We are what we think. To change what we are, we
have to change what we think. But to change what
we think, we have to know what we think and that
is not as easy as it sounds because the ruts were laid
down in a time beyond memory.

As a start on discovering the first ruts, it sometimes helps to do as simple a thing as making a list: The world is . . . People are . . . I am . . . I fear . . . Mothers are . . . Fathers are . . . Friends are . . . Bosses are . . . Writing off the top of one's head, as rapidly and "thoughtlessly" as possible, may allow some surprising things to slip through, providing a glimpse of the unconscious beliefs that influence, or even dominate, one's behavior.

If Poppy were capable of making such a list, it might read like this. People are . . . loud, careless, threatening, unpredictable, mean, cruel, murderous. I fear . . . being unloved, abandoned, hurt, destroyed. I must always be . . . careful, guarded, defended, hidden. I wonder, though, if Poppy could have gotten through even this short a list without thinking: *But this person where I am now has never hit me, never yelled at me or thrown me around like a beanbag or locked me out all night.* Noticing the contradiction, perhaps she would then have the courage to test the possibility that her beliefs made perfectly good sense once upon a time but that once upon a time was not now.

Recently I had a cyst removed that, inside me, was a hard and sizable lump. The surgeon placed it on a piece of gauze and showed it to me. To my surprise, as large as it had felt, it was only the size of a green pea. The surgeon then stuck it with his scalpel and it was gone, collapsed, nothing left behind but a stain on the gauze. Just so, beliefs, hard and sizable inside, may collapse when brought to the outside and subjected to reality, leaving only traces of themselves behind.

Not all of them will disappear, only the ones that anyone, even the invested self, can see are outmoded and ridiculous. Some more, with honest effort, can be traced to their origins and then discarded on the basis of: that was then and this is now. And some will stubbornly remain because we are attached to our explanations about the world and the people in it, but with luck they may slowly grow less influential.

We do not really like to look at what we think for fear of bringing up frightening and unpleasant memories. Looming as a danger also is the fact that we may have to start behaving differently, and it is an effort and a nuisance to learn new ways; the old ways, however destructive to peace and happiness, are nevertheless comfortable in their familiarity. But when there has been a crippling of the self-esteem because of early experiences, when a life is being lived without freedom, without expansiveness, without happiness, when it is being lived in a dark hole, it *is* worth making an effort.

It has occurred to me lately that many people may realize they were provided with a faulty map at the beginning of their journey through life but our current culture of victimization encourages them not to take responsibility for correcting it and instead to spend their time blaming the mapmakers. "My mother didn't love me." "My father didn't spend any time with me," they say. "I was abused." "I was neglected." "My parents expected too much." "My parents expected too little." "My parents didn't speak." "My parents fought all the time." Trashing parents has become virtually the national pastime.

We all find it easy to cite chapter and verse of what our parents did wrong that explains, and excuses, the way we are now. What we usually fail to take into account, though, is that our parents did not set out with the intention of providing a faulty map. I doubt that any man and woman ever got together and said, "Let's make a baby so we have someone to beat up on" or neglect or smother or confuse or frighten or hurt, or whatever. It happens. It happens all the time. But not by design. It happens because parents do not know or cannot do better.

A cat could hardly have had a worse start in life than Poppy did, but the children from up the road did not pummel her and toss and tease her and lock her out at night in order to make her fear the world and devalue herself. They did these things because that was the way they were at that stage of their lives. If she could express blame, Poppy would be right to point to them as the reason for her hiding out in a black hole. But however satisfying that might be, pointing to them would do nothing at all to liberate her from the hole. She could rage over what was done to her. She could weep for the past and her unhappy childhood. She could blame the circumstances she was unlucky enough to be born into. But it would still be she who was in the hole, until and unless she took responsibility for getting out of it.

But she never did. When Socksie found his way to GoWell, Poppy ventured forth from her hole hours at a time to lie close to him, and she became even more attached to Trot when he arrived. Although Poppy must have been aware of the ease of her fellow cats, she remained loyal to her distorted views and any slight disturbance sent her racing back to the cellar. In her imagination the tigers still roared and she never made herself hold still long enough to recognize that they were paper tigers.

"Observe and endure" is the favorite phrase of a psychotherapist who is also a practitioner of Zen Buddhism. "Observe and endure," he advises when a situation is unclear and anxiety-provoking, by which he means observe the situation to see how it differs from the past and endure the anxiety while you try out different behaviors to see if they are not more appropriate than the old learned responses. In other words, hang in there until you see whether you are dealing with real tigers or only paper ones from the past.

A new little kitten named Natty Bumppo is currently doing just that. I was up on the mountain road on my motor scooter last summer, with Charlie running alongside me. Charlie is Freebie's successor, as Freebie was Hector's. Freebie, too, had her problems with the past. Some months after we got her, she developed a lump on her side—nothing serious; a fatty tumor—but it seemed best to have it removed, and we took her to the animal hospital. She was frantic at being left because the previous time she had been handed over to strangers and put in a cage, it had been the end of her known world. Apparently desperately afraid of a second such loss, she struggled so against the anesthetic that she went into cardiac arrest on the operating table and died.

Thus it was Charlie, black and white like Freebie but as large as Hector, who caught sight of movement in tall grass, investigated, and tumbled a tiny kitten out into the road. The kitten tried gamely to stave Charlie off by hissing and arching her back, substantiating a comment I recently read that, when frightened, a child runs to an adult for protection, a puppy grovels, but a kitten stands its ground and puts up a fight. I captured the kitten and examined her.

Pathetically thin and with her tail smashed in two places as though it had been slammed in a door, she was not an irresistible kitten, but I could not leave her there. She was starving and much too young to have a chance of surviving on her own, so I popped her into the basket on the handlebars of my scooter, whistled to Charlie, and dropped down the mountain to GoWell.

Connie called her Natty Bumppo, and the name, since Bumpy suited the state of her tail, stuck. Bumpy was as traumatized as Poppy had been and she spent her early time with us being fearful, but unlike Poppy, she was able to observe and endure. Each week she came out of hiding for a longer period. Each week she endured our gentle stroking for a longer time. After a while she had observed us long enough to risk claiming a high windowsill in the downstairs bathroom as her special place from which to watch the birds at the feeders in the chokecherry trees. The windowsill is at head height, which meant that whenever Connie or I went in the bathroom, we gave her a kiss. At first, she fled, then she endured, then she responded, and now, if either of us appears, she stretches out to kiss us, bumping her forehead against our cheeks and rubbing the sides of our faces.

Bumpy took a risk. She hung in and tested her fears, and now that she knows they are groundless, she has changed and become trusting. She has a fine start on a good life.

Sometimes I think the riskiest thing one can do is not to take a risk. I see it in the garden: things that do not grow do not just stay the same; they die back little by little. But if you do take a risk, if you observe and endure and try new ways of being, your wound can become your capital, which is to say that the lacerating things that happened can be the source of valuable qualities.

The people I know who are the most creative, the most insightful, curious, and alert, the ones who seek and delve and struggle to understand, are the ones who were wounded when young. When I was in college, I envied a girl in my dormitory who often talked of her loving parents and idyllic childhood until one day I realized that, of us all, she was the least interesting person. There was a complacency and placidity about her that made her a person without sides, without edges. She was pleasant to be with, but she was not exciting or stimulating or in the least original. It was the people scarred by private wars who were the most dimensional. It was their wounds that constituted the capital they drew on to feed their talents, to provide grounds for empathy and spur for achievement.

For you or me to be the particular person each of us is, nothing could have been different in our pasts. We could not have had different parents or different experiences or we would not be the people we are. Thus, it does not make any sense to regret the past. The only thing we can rightfully deplore is the attitudes we developed based on that past, and those are within our power to change if we explore the ruts our thinking follows, forgive the people who sent us down wrong roads, and observe and endure as we try out new ways of being in the world. Our early autobiographies will remain the same, but their power to bind us to old and outmoded ways will be ended.

For five or six years nothing but good came Poppy's way. She had a house to live in. She had all she wanted to eat. She was tended when she was sick. There was catnip to roll in and strings to play with, a large property to roam and a field to hunt in. There were Trot and Socksie to be her friends. But Poppy never let go of her fear of being mistreated.

For a reason to be explained, eventually we had to get Trot out of the house. An acquaintance with a horse farm volunteered that Trot could live in the stables where there were other cats and stablehands to keep them supplied with Cat Chow and water. It was either that or have Trot put down, so we gratefully accepted the offer and asked if Poppy could go with him because they were attached to each other. We thought it might console Trot for his exile and would make little difference to Poppy since she lived in the cellar anyway.

After Trot and Poppy were released in the stable, Poppy was sighted streaking across the pasture. And no one ever saw her again. So, in the end, Poppy was right: the world was cruel and no one cared about her.

We live our beliefs about the world, good or bad,
and the beliefs become the reality of our lives, good
or bad. We think the world is this way or that, and
in the long run it always proves to be exactly the
way we think it is. Good or bad.

Chester

Books on cat care set out clear instructions on the way a new cat should be introduced into the household. If the newcomer is a stray, the books recommend that he be quarantined for several days, isolated in a bathroom or spare room with food, water, and a litter box, and only gradually introduced to the other pets in the household. But I cannot do this. Even if I had the heart to shut a frightened cat up alone, my experience is that the resident cats spend those several days sniffing at the crack under the door and working up a fearsome hatred of the creature on the other side, while for his part the new cat is coming to believe that dragons inhabit the house. Better to get the introductions over with at once, I feel, when the resident cats are as startled by the entrance of the newcomer as he is by being in a strange place and none have had time to work out reasons for not getting along.

Accordingly, when Connie and I picked up Chester in the parking lot and brought him home late on a Saturday night, we simply set him down inside the front door and left him free to explore. His nose informed him that fellow creatures had recently bestirred the air and he advanced to the kitchen as only a cat can, leaning backward while creeping forward, but neither my Kate nor Connie's Pickles put in an appearance, so Chester, like Goldilocks, had leisure in which to sample their food bowls and try out their perching places.

Kate and Pickles discovered him in the morning. Growls and hisses blackened the air. The new cat met the tainted greetings with such an air of dignity and reserve, merely sitting up straighter and weaving his head to dodge attempts to cuff him, that the home cats soon tired of the attempt to intimidate him and moved on to the more interesting question of what was being offered them for breakfast.

In the daylight, we saw that the newcomer was not so much ginger-colored as blond, a creamy beige longhair with a white shirtfront, white tufts between his toes and in his ears, sweeping white whiskers, a luxuriant tail, and clear amber eyes. While not a thoroughbred Persian, Chester surely was the near relative of one.

"How are you this morning?" we asked. "You

look less lost but not very much at home." Although
we patted him lightly, neither Connie nor I picked
the cat up, I suppose because he seemed so reserved,
so held within himself. He gave the impression of
being unexacting, leaving it to us to decide whether
or not to like him, whether or not to take an interest in his fate. Connie made calls to the police and
the animal welfare officer in the township. No one
had yet reported a missing butterscotch cat, so,
beyond leaving telephone numbers and his description, there was little more that we could do.

Friends came by that afternoon, and as we went in
and out to the terrace, the screen door swung wide
and Chester slipped through. A guest pointed to
him as he vanished around a corner of the house.
Connie was busy inside, and before I could start
after him, he had melted away into wild rose thickets bordering a creek on the far side of the house and
was almost certainly beyond retrieving. Just to be
sure, I circled around and walked a bit of the way up
the mountain road.

I was about to turn back when I caught sight of
him. He was moving resolutely along the creek bed,
headed in the general direction of the town of
Chester. The creek bank was too steep and over-
grown for me to go after him, but I could keep pace
with him on the road. I thought it might frighten
him into running if I called. Instead, I talked softly
and slowly, as if to myself, just to let him know I
was there.

"Good kitty, it's miles to Chester. It's so far that you'll have to go to houses on the way and ask to be taken in and fed and have the burrs combed out of your fur. You really would be better off to stay with us. We're trying to find your people for you, and if we don't, Connie will take you and you can live in a grand apartment on Fifth Avenue."

The underbrush thinned out. The cat had a clear course either way, over open fields to the left in the direction of Chester or to the right to the road and me. He hesitated. I went on talking. He looked toward Chester. Then, as though relinquishing that past life, he turned slowly, crossed the creek on rocks, climbed the bank, came to me, and allowed himself to be picked up. My impression was not so much that he wished to stay as that he was too polite to go, that he could not bring himself to be so rude, when I was speaking to him, as to turn his back and walk away.

Does it seem strange to credit a cat with good manners? Connie, too, was soon remarking on the courteousness of this cat. When no owner turned up to claim him, she took Chester to New York with her. Since Pickles rightfully regarded Connie's apartment as her territory, she frequently hissed her displeasure at Chester's presence and rushed at him like a farmer's wife bent on shooing chickens out of the vegetable garden. Chester accepted the unprovoked assaults in silence, waiting politely until Pickles regained her composure and then continuing on his way. This at first made Pickles even more irritable—she was probably itching for a noisy, fur-flying fight to establish who was top cat—but as she came more and more to realize that Chester never intended to dispute her for the position, she ended by growing a little fond of him and swiped at him only when she was feeling more paranoid than usual.

Unlike other cats, who, in someone's amusing description, do not come when you call but take a message and get back to you, as soon as Chester learned his name, he invariably answered promptly to it, but he clearly preferred not to be picked up or held. When he was, he endured the handling patiently and even purred in response to being talked to. He never squirmed or scratched in an effort to be put down, nor did he stiffen his legs to push one's face away if he was being held upside down and given a nose rub. At most, a plaintive lit-tle cry escaped him if the demonstration of affection went on too long.

When a three-year-old child came on a visit, Chester was the only cat polite enough not to hide, which meant that he was clutched around the mid-dle and lugged to and fro most of the day. Had it been any other cat, we would have snatched it away for fear of the child's being bitten or scratched, but we knew the little girl was safe with Chester. His good manners never deserted him. He was a cat very easy to get along with, a cat that other cats and peo-ple liked and trusted.

Manners have that reassuring effect. Like the center white line on a road, they make behavior predictable, avert collisions, and keep things running smoothly, whether the possessor of them is a cat or a person. It seems regrettable that, in the name of individuality and freedom, manners are being swept away. We less and less do the civilized thing, more and more do our own thing. Curiously enough, it seems to me that the effect is not to make people more relaxed and spontaneous but less so, for in the absence of generally agreed-upon standards of behavior to act as white lines, we have to be on guard to protect our person, our property, and our prerogatives. The world is less pleasant, less ordered, and staying safe in it requires a degree of attention that used to be free to go in more rewarding directions.

People who still value manners in this land of instant intimacy necessarily seem a bit formal. Upon meeting another person, they do not presume to become immediate buddies. They are not eager to know or be known until there has been time to determine whether they like the person, whether they will get along. They do not commit themselves until there is trust and mutuality. So it was with Chester. He was a long time in committing himself to Connie, and after Connie and he and Pickles came to GoWell to live, to me.

Like people who are reserved, Chester needed to

be sure of barriers before he could build bridges. He needed to be sure his boundaries would be acknowledged before he could give up defending them. There was no way of knowing what Chester's early life had been, but he had the air of a cat who was used to doing without closeness, as though he had been on his own as long as he could remember, cared for but not cared about.

Although he never voluntarily settled himself in a lap, Chester was not antisocial. He did not go off by himself but spent his evenings in the living room and broke into a loud, rumbling purr when spoken to. He was companionable but as sufficient unto himself as a mountain village, happy to accept attention but never in need of it, never seeking it.

The more I came to know Chester, the more he reminded me of a bachelor, the type of man I imagine almost everyone has known at one time or another; that is, someone charming, witty, attractive, often helpful and warm and easy to be with, but a loner, not in the Western sense of a cowboy drifting from place to place but in the sense of dodging ultimate commitment. I wonder if that bedrock separateness is why bachelors have a reputation as heartbreakers? The ones I have known have been such delightful company that inevitable fantasies of having found the right man begin to surface, the right man for yourself if you are unattached or for a sister, daughter, or friend. But nothing comes of your introductions or of your own efforts, and

because the man is so well put together, you assume
that you, or whoever, is not good enough, not
engaging or attractive or compelling enough to cap-
ture his deeper affection, and you weep for the failure. Now I know, partially because I observed it
with Chester, that the relationship never deepens or
ripens because such a person is preserving his safety
zone. The zone is not wide, it is invisible, almost
undetectable, but it is uncrossable. Where does it
come from? Why is it needed?

The single hint Chester gave us about his previous
life was his liking for newspapers and brown paper
bags. If we could not find that day's newspaper, it
was under Chester. If we picked up a seemingly
empty grocery sack and found it unexpectedly
heavy, it was because Chester was curled in the bottom of it. This liking for papers and bags suggested
that he had been a store cat, in which case an emotional self-sufficiency had been required of him. If
we were right about this, he was in the constant
presence of people coming and going but in intimate relationship to none. He might be petted and
praised for his looks, but it would be only a momen-
tary contact, with never enough time to learn to love
and trust. What he did learn was that, no matter
how many people were around, he was essentially
alone; no matter how many people patted his head,
none were available when he needed arms and a lap.
His emotional sustenance had to come from within.

People who are detached, who steer clear of closeness and relationships of any intensity, have perhaps grown up in an analogous situation: for instance, busy parents who come and go with little more than a pat on the head for the child; a mother who makes her child into a parent to look after her; an alcoholic parent who needs frequent picking up and dusting off; an absent or departed parent—any situation in which the child has had to grow up in a hurry and take responsibility rather than having responsibility taken for him/her. The child early learns to go it alone. He/she cannot later unlearn it.

There is an admirable quality about such people, as there was about Chester. They tend to handle their lives well, with a minimum of fuss. Their egos need little cosseting. They come across as well-wrapped packages, not ones with burst seams and contents oozing out. Because they have not put all their chips on that one other person, on that one intimate relationship, they are likely to have many and varied friendships and to be much in demand socially. One thinks of novelist Henry James and his dining out every night during the London social season.

Are such people to be pitied because they do not know what it is to be part of the oneness of two, the inimitable closeness of a marriage or long-term relationship? Yes and no. No and yes. Love is incomparable in its possibilities, but its possibilities are so seldom delightfully realized that a life without it may be as much a blessing as curse. And a life without it certainly need not lack for meaning and strong satisfactions.

Chester found meaning and satisfaction in the same place that people so often find it: in work. Our present-day thinking lauds personal relationships, time and again citing them as the area that makes life worthwhile. But work, work that is worth doing and that one does at the top of one's bent, is also profoundly gratifying. As engrossing as love, challenging work does not use up what it feeds on, as love tends to do, but instead grows in interest and rewards, opening out and leading on. It makes exciting use of one's energies and intellect. It provides a place to be and someone to be. It is the armature on which the clay of lives is shaped.

The work Chester elected for himself was hunting. He set out in the morning and was gone most of the day, gone in the sense that he was around the grounds, where we occasionally saw and spoke to him, but he did not return to the house until dinnertime. He scorned the easy task of lurking under the bird feeders in favor of watching one or another bed of pachysandra or myrtle for the slight twitches that hinted a rodent was moving about underneath or crouching motionless on a rock wall staring at a gap where a chipmunk might appear or prowling the woods skirting the back of the property on the lookout for squirrels or rabbits. Many a time I saw him emerge from the woods, highstepping down

the path, head held awkwardly high to avoid tripping on his catch, and I knew he had captured a
garter snake. There the little snake would hang, a
limp circle dangling from Chester's mouth.

He would set down his catch, almost always completely unharmed, near to a person if one was about
or on the front walk and watch benevolently as the
creature decided on a course of action. Mice, seemingly stunned by their good fortune in being released,
stayed unmoving for many seconds, then gathered
their wits and made a dash for it. Chipmunks, for
their part, immediately began a circular dance of the
handicapped. The first time I saw this performance
I thought Chester had caused some neurological
damage, for the chipmunk lurched in a circle, its
head bent far to the side, dragging one leg and making strange little aimless hops and jumps. But when
I bent to pick it up, my touch galvanized it into a
straight dash for cover. After I observed other cap-

tured chipmunks going through the same gyrations, it dawned on me that this must be a charade intended to convince the captor that his prey was mortally wounded and he could relax his vigilance, thus allowing the chipmunk a chance to escape. Snakes, on the other hand, moved not at all but lay perfectly lifeless even when Chester nudged them with a paw. Fortunately, before I knew of this propensity to sham death, I was squeamish enough not to pick the snake up to dispose of it. Instead, I got a rake and hooked it with a tine. The snake promptly curled around the tine and darted its tongue at me, so I knew not to drop it in the river but to set it free in the field across the road.

Chester's intent was not to kill or devour but to engage in the work of capturing the creatures. It was what he did. After he had shown us his catch with evident pride, like a fisherman releasing a trout back into the stream, he was content to let the creature go free. The benefits he got from his work were, I think, much the same benefits that people get from their work. It gave him confidence in his own abilities. It organized his time. It lent meaning to his life.

American Impressionist painter Mary Cassatt once wrote in a letter to her brother, "I work, and that is the whole secret of anything like content in life." I thought of this a few days ago when I was standing in line at the post office behind a slouching, leather-jacketed fellow who was greeted by a friend.

"Hey, buddy, how ya doin'? Ya workin'?"

"Ya nuts?" the fellow said scornfully, and went on to brag that his mother kept him supplied with pocket money. "Let her hold down the crummy job," he said. "Work is for suckers."

I had a strong urge to tap the guy on the shoulder and say, "You can't imagine how wrong you are. Work is the meaty part of life, the part you can sink your teeth into and get real nourishment from."

He would not have believed me, of course, because work has a poor reputation. It is what humankind has supposedly been cursed with since the days of Cain and Abel. It is what people plan to escape from into retirement. It is why people play the lottery or scheme to make millions in the market, so they will no longer have to work. In some parts of the world, work is a dreadful burden, of course, and in this country, too, in the mills and factories, it was once a matter of long hours, inhuman conditions, and relentless exploitation. But the unions changed that. Workers organized and won reasonable working hours and work rules describing the limits of what they could be required to do. This was immensely to the good, but then the law of unintended consequences kicked in. In the fight against the exploitation of workers, work itself came to be seen as exploitative and the idea spread that the ideal setup was to do as little of it as possible.

I once worked at a publishing firm with a fellow who felt that way. Our job was to edit medical text-books, but Hank spent major portions of his day reading novels concealed in his desk drawer. When the boss came by, he slid the drawer closed and looked up, pencil in hand, a slight frown of concentration on his face as though pondering the placement of a comma. Actually, Hank did not much care where commas went and even less about medical texts. His interest was in outwitting the owner of the company, who wanted the most work for the least amount of money, by supplying him with the least work for the most money. If I had been keeping score, I would have said that Hank came out ahead of the owner. But he lost a great deal more than he won. While the rest of us working there learned an astonishing amount of medicine and were often engrossed by the texts we edited, Hank, skimming the manuscripts, was chronically bored and irritated. He found the work unchallenging because all he did was keep an eye out for misspelled words, while the rest of us found it complex because we closely followed the concepts under discussion. We were involved and got a lot out of the work; Hank was uninvolved and tried to get out of a lot of the work.

"It is not hard work which is dreary; it is superficial work," remarked classical scholar Edith Hamilton, to which I would add: "Or work done superficially." The best part of engaging yourself fully with your work is losing yourself in it. So long ago that I no longer remember whose comment it was, a writer said that when he was working, first the world in general left his room, then his family and friends, then the critics, and on good days, when his work was going really well, he himself left the room, meaning that he was lost in his work, he was unaware of himself; he had floated free of his own concerns. Anne Morrow Lindbergh in *Gift from the Sea* put it this way: "What release to write so that one forgets oneself, forgets one's companion, forgets where one is or what one is going to do next—to be drenched in work as one is drenched in sleep or in the sea."

The experience is incomparable, and it is not in the least confined to writers. Scientists, steelworkers, carpenters, painters, mechanics and engineers, landscapers, musicians—anyone passionately engaged in making, designing, discovering, repairing, or creating—can find at any moment that everyone else has gone out of his space and he is at the center of his world. That is why work is such a great anesthetic for pain, the most effective antidote for disappointment, despair, or despondency, the best means of coping with tragedy. "Work is the most efficient anodyne," Leonard Woolf observed in his autobiography, ". . . whether the pain be in your great toe, your teeth, your head, or your heart." I saw the truth of this when I visited my sister in the hospital. The patient in the next bed had had a manhole cover, blown off by steam, strike her in the face. In the midst of the psychic pain of disfigurement and the physical pain of a series of plastic surgeries, she found hours of forgetfulness each day through passionate absorption in her work of designing kitchens.

People are most successful in their pursuit of happiness when they realize the happiness there is in pursuit.

Have I overdone my enthusiasm for work? Very likely, for I do feel strongly about it, although no more so than the unknown person who wrote the following:

If you are poor, work. If you are rich, work. If you are burdened with seemingly unfair responsibilities, work.

If you are happy, continue to work; idleness gives room for doubts and fears. If sorrow overwhelms you, and loved ones seem not true, work. If disappointments come, work.

If faith falters and reason fails, just work. When dreams are shattered and hopes seem dead—work, work as if your life were in peril; it really is.

No matter what ails you, work. Work faithfully, and work with faith. Work is the greatest material remedy available. Work will cure both mental and physical affliction.

Chester was, I think, the most serious cat I have known, keeping his dignity fairly well intact even when rolling in catnip, which he was exceedingly fond of and asked for daily by sitting in front of the drawer where it was kept, occasionally looking over his shoulder to note whether the passing person realized he was waiting for his treat. There was one occasion, however, when Chessie entirely slipped his character bonds and became a free spirit.

Connie and I were driving to New York on a

Sunday night. Chester was in his carrier, Pickles in hers, the radio was on, and I began singing to the music. The song was "Alice Blue Gown," and on the second chorus suddenly Chessie lifted his head, opened his mouth, and howled the melody. We were dumbstruck. We applauded. We cheered. We

laughed. Never before had he done anything like it. And never again did he do it. The possible explanation for this one time was proposed by Connie.

"You were so far off-key that he couldn't stand it,"

she said. I had to admit that Chessie had done what anyone near me does when I sing: try to drown me out or nudge me onto the melody by example. It is bad enough to be tone-deaf, but to be corrected by a cat . . . !

But I forgave him and loved Chessie all the same, and he did not hold my singing against me. On hot summer afternoons when he came along the path out of the woods and spotted me on my knees weeding, he speeded up and came quick and straight to me, speaking throatily with rumblings and gruff cries of delight—in himself, the day, life, and the world—and bumping his face against mine in ecstasies of affection. He never did anything of the sort indoors, but in the garden on hands and knees, I was close to his level; he had easy access to me of his own volition, and he knew I would not reach for him, would not touch him because my hands were in the dirt, would not hold him when he wished to go. Knowing that he was free to go, he became free to stay.

In the garden he had his distance, and it was then that Chester felt safe to cross the distance and express all the affection buried deep within him.

Socksie

On a winter evening some years ago Connie and I were having dinner with neighbors. The dining table was in a windowed alcove, and as we sat there in the radiance of candlelight, hot food on the table and glowing wine in the glasses, a scrawny black cat with white socks and shirt and a battle-nicked ear leaped out of the black night onto the outside windowsill. Yearning toward the warmth and the food, he opened his mouth wide in cries muffled to soundlessness by the double thickness of the storm windows.

Connie made a move to get up, but Sergio, our host, shook his head. "Not ours," he said. "One of Cleefie Beam's."

"But Cleefie's been gone a year," Connie said. Cleefie was an old man, illiterate and occasionally irascible, who had lived in a one-room shack on a pond across the road from the neighbors. Existing on white bread, baked beans, tobacco, and beer, when he got too blind to distinguish even light and dark, a son showed up to retrieve him from the shack, and the shack was now a pile of rubble, kicked down by vandals.

"Outside cat," said Sergio dismissively, implying that as long as the creature at the window was not accustomed to being inside, it could perfectly well survive what was rapidly turning into the coldest night of the year. "Ciao!" he yelled, rapping on the window to scare the wraith away. Sergio was Italian and wasted no more sentiment on animals than Cleefie's son had, or, for that matter, Cleefie himself. I had stopped to say hello to the old man one day and been horrified by the blood-swollen ticks on the faces of several kittens playing at his feet. When I asked why he didn't pull the ticks off, Cleefie answered indifferently that they would fall off when they were through feeding on the kittens' blood.

Jane, Sergio's wife, returned from a trip to the kitchen bearing hot rolls. She too shrugged when she saw the cat. Since we could not invite a stray into someone else's home, there was nothing Connie or I could do, and by the time we said good night and walked to GoWell along the snow-crusted road, the cat had disappeared.

We did not see the cat again until spring, when we occasionally glimpsed one or more of Cleefie's abandoned cats ducking into holes under the rubble of the shack or getting a drink at the edge of the pond. Because they vanished at the sound of a foot-step and were obviously fending for themselves, we assumed they wished for no human intervention in their lives, except, perhaps, on a bitterly cold night, and we made no attempt to approach them.

That summer and another winter went by before one of the cats began turning up near GoWell. We heard him long before we saw him. He had a harsh, rasping voice, perhaps from inhaling Cleefie Beam's pipe smoke when he was a kitten, and he called urgently but a little plaintively to our cats from somewhere in the woods, as though he wished for their company but was afraid to come closer to seek it out. One day, when both Connie and I were in the garden but out of sight on our hands and knees, he came strolling along the ridge of the old railroad track and we got a look at him: he was skin and bones, a dusty, frowzy black cat with such a wasted body that his head looked huge in comparison. Because he had the same white paws, white chest, and notched ear, we recognized him as the cat on the windowsill of two winters before and were glad to see he was still surviving. We made a move to fetch food for him but he fled when he caught sight of us.

The next afternoon he returned, calling as he

came along the ridge. "Come to think of it," I remarked to Connie, "I haven't seen any cats around Cleefie's old place since I don't know when. I wonder if this is the only one left and he's lonely?"

He sounded lonely. Although his yellow eyes glared and he looked fierce and wild, there was something wistful in the way he called to our cats and watched from a distance as they lounged on the grass. He was like an orphan looking on at a happy family scene. But again he vanished when we approached, so there was nothing we could do about him.

On a Sunday evening a week or two later, we were packed and ready to leave for New York. All we had still to do was to bundle Chester and Pickles and Poppy into their carriers—Kate, who had been traveling since she was a kitten, rode free. The other three hated being transported and went into deep and cunning hiding the minute they suspected it was Sunday night, a habit we headed off by shutting them in the downstairs bathroom before we started loading the car. On this particular evening, when we went into the bathroom to pack them up, Pickles bolted through Connie's legs and was out the front door before we could catch her. In a flash she disappeared under the porch, diving through a cat-sized triangle where the steps met the mainframe. To retrieve her was impossible, to tempt her out unlikely now that she had the wind up. We had no choice but to leave her behind. We filled a large

Pyrex bowl with cat crackers, a second one with water, crossed our fingers that she would survive the week on her own, and drove off.

When the car headlights hit the front porch the following Friday night, there was Pickles—and a second body streaked into the night, a black body with white socks. The wild cat, perhaps sniffing out the bowl of crackers, had raised enough courage to come to the house. After that, I took to leaving a bowl of crackers for him on the porch every Sunday night, and when summer came and I stayed on at the house for weeks at a time, I filled the bowl each evening.

One night I heard a thump on the porch. After a second and third loud thump, I looked out, expecting to see the black cat. Instead, a large possum was munching away, occasionally putting his front paws on the rim of the bowl to tip it and spill crackers onto the porch and then letting it go so that the bowl rocked back upright with a thump. When I looked out a bit later, the place of the large possum had been taken by a midsize possum, and later still it was a baby possum who was there. I was feeding the whole family. But since I also occasionally glimpsed the black cat and he looked a little less emaciated, I gathered he was managing to get a share of the food.

One hot summer morning I propped the cellar door open to let air circulate through the house. In the afternoon when I went upstairs on an errand, as I put my foot on the top step an animal hurtled past me, flying with such speed that I doubt it touched a step all the way down. I arrived at a window in time to see the black cat bolting out of the cellar and around the corner of the house. In the bedroom Poppy and Pickles, each on a twin bed, were sitting upright looking startled at the commotion. Not only was Poppy not in the cellar, which was surprising in itself, but next to her was a rumpled indentation in the white candlewick bedspread and a faint haze of black fur. The black cat had found his way in, made friends with Poppy, and the two of them had been taking their ease.

The next afternoon when I went upstairs, his departure at the sound of my footsteps was somewhat less precipitous. In fact, when the cat saw that I did not intend to hit him, his feet slowed and his exit took on a distinctly reluctant cast. The following afternoon he merely sat up on the bed and stared at me with his wide yellow eyes, ready to do battle if he had to but a little hopeful.

"It's all right," I said. "You can sleep here if you like."

The cat watched with tense caution while I went about my business. I ignored him and as the minutes went by, his eyelids began to drift closed and he subsided into the hollow he had made on the bed. It must have been a luxury for him not only to be cushioned and comfortable but to feel himself safe from predators, and he was soon snoringly deep in sleep.

From coming into the house to sleep away the afternoons, it was a short step to staying for meals. I rather suspect the black cat felt he had lucked into paradise, for a bowl of dry food was always available at the cat commissary in the hallway off the kitchen and often enough the other cats had left behind bits, chunks, or whole dishes of canned food because a flavor they had loved yesterday was somehow not acceptable today. The black cat could hardly believe his eyes that so much food was to be had for the taking, and at least once a day he seriously overate, threw up, and returned immediately to eat more. Although I did not appreciate it when the throwing up took place on the kitchen floor, I figured that a cat brave enough and resourceful enough to stay alive for several years on his own deserved a chance at the life of Riley while he had it. It would not last, for come fall, I would be returning to New York.

This was one of the reasons I did not give him a name. He spent only afternoons in the house, and since I was seldom inside in the summer, our acquaintance was casual and wary. Neither of us was quite sure about the other's behavior, he because I was a human, I because he was fierce-looking, but even if he hadn't returned to the wild each night, I would not have adopted him because I had Kate and Poppy and the golden retriever to take back and forth on weekends and was firm against adding to that number. So, he went nameless until the day he caught sight of me kneeling in the garden and hastened so purposefully toward me, his white knee-highs flashing like scissor blades, that I involuntarily said, "Hello there, Socks." All right, Socksie was a generic name for any cat with white feet. It was so unimaginative that to call him Socksie did not make him my cat. It was just something to refer to him by.

September came and home base shifted back to the city. Socksie looked on wistfully as I packed the car on Sunday nights, and when I returned on Friday, he was either waiting on the porch or turned up early Saturday morning. One Sunday evening I left the car door open while I ran back in the house for one last bag. On my return, about to slam the door, I spotted Socksie inside the car. He was crouched on top of Poppy's carrier, his white paws hidden under his body as though he were trying to make himself all black to escape detection. But he could not resist turning his yellow questing eyes on me to see whether I was going to throw him out or take him along to wherever it was the animals and I went when we left him behind.

"No, Socksie," I said. "I can't. I can't have one more cat to carry back and forth. Besides, you wouldn't like being cooped up in a city apartment."

I lifted him. He groaned and rammed his head under my chin. I had never clipped his claws, not only because he needed them for protection but because I was afraid of his wildness, and now he used them to clutch at my sleeve. "I'm sorry, Socksie," I said, disengaging them. "Your crackers are on the porch. We'll be back Friday. You'll be all right."

I thought about him during the week, about his having dared to get in the car. It must have taken real courage, for he had spent his life fleeing from cars and people. He had risked everything in an effort to belong.

The next weekend he did not leave the house at

sundown but instead ventured into the living room and looked long and hard at Connie and me as we sat having a drink before dinner. Slowly he moved in front of me, sat, and studied my face. He moved closer and put a paw on the edge of the chair. When I said nothing, he inched himself up onto the chair and crouched. I stroked his back lightly. Revving up his purr, which was the roar of a pebbled beach tumbling in the wake of a wave, he insinuated himself into my lap. Getting bolder with each passing moment and purring ever louder, he stretched until he could wedge his head under my chin, and there he settled.

"He's won," I said to Connie. "I want him to be an outside cat, but he wants to be an inside cat and he's won."

"I thought he would," she smiled.

Socksie reminded me of a newspaper editor I had known years before in London who wanted to marry a woman who was in love with a foreign correspondent. The glamorous correspondent had a way of turning up from Africa or the Far East just when the steady guy seemed to be gaining ground. Each time it was back to square one for the faithful suitor, but he never gave up. He didn't act vexed; he didn't protest playing second fiddle; he just kept on being there, and eventually a time came when the correspondent stayed away too long and the woman married the man who loved her. There is much to be said for persistence.

Friendships can come about by this same agency of one person's being, not a nuisance, but persevering. In an advertising agency where I was employed after I left the publishing company, a copywriter was hired who was sharply intelligent and crisp to the point of being hard-edged. I was slightly in awe of her and uncomfortable in her company, which made me reluctant to respond to indications that she would like to make friends. But she abided, accepting my refusal of invitations with equanimity but trying again after a lulling interval. It was a couple of years before she succeeded in making even a passing friend of me, but, like Socksie, she persisted— in both instances, to my great benefit, for I ended up having my life enriched by the person and the cat alike.

More recently, it is I who have been persistent. After moving to the country, I read an article in the local paper about a couple with interests similar to mine. I found a mutual friend to introduce us and we spent a pleasant evening in company. After that . . . nothing. They were leading full lives and had no need of another person in them. But just as the woman in the office knew that she would be a good friend to me, so I knew I would be a good friend to them. It took a long time, but I persisted and now we have a true and valued friendship.

Socksie had a difficult start in life. Poppy had a difficult start in life. The difference between them was that Socksie never gave up on the future. Instead of being deformed by circumstance, as Poppy was, he remained interested in his fate and optimistic about its betterment, and this is, I suspect, the secret to mastering trauma.

I once lost someone who meant the world to me and it was a struggle not to despair, but I tried to remain interested in what was happening to me instead of being defeated by it. I reminded myself that this life, however grisly it was at the moment, was the only life I would ever have. I would not be granted a chance to do it over and make it come out right next time, so I had to find a way to make it work this time if once more it was to be a pleasure instead of an affliction.

I had lived long enough by then to know that around the next corner, or the next, or the one after that, things usually take a turn for the better. If you keep going, if you keep your head unbowed however bloody it may be, if you never, never give up, sooner or later new paths open into new landscapes you have no knowledge of at the moment. It is the one thing you can be sure of about life: good or bad, it will change.

One of my early part-time jobs was typing reports for a psychologist who was a specialist in the Projective Techniques, such as the Rorschach, TAT, and Szondi tests. Patients were sent to her by psychiatrists and psychoanalysts for diagnosis at the beginning of treatment, much as patients are sent for X rays to aid in the diagnosis of physical symptoms. Fifteen years into her practice, the psychologist decided to conduct a follow-up study, retesting some seven hundred patients to see if she could determine which type of therapy was most efficacious with which type of patient. To her surprise, she discovered that the best therapist was life, the most effective therapy a positive change in life circumstances. Persons who had separated from parents and gone off to college, or left a failed marriage and gotten a divorce, or quit a despised job for one more to their liking, or moved from the country to the city or the city to the country, persons who had succeeded in establishing their own business, who had left an abusive situation, who had been freed by the death of a parent or partner from a love-hate relationship—whatever the positive change, it was these people who showed the greatest and most lasting psychological change.

Is the moral of that: don't go to a psychotherapist; instead, change your circumstances? I imagine it is if you are like Socksie and can hold on to your equilibrium and optimism through the bad times until a path opens to a new life. But it is probably not if, like Poppy, you interpret changed circumstances, even ones changed much for the better, in the same old way and react to them in the same old way. Then it is not circumstances but you who need to change, and for that, psychotherapy may be indicated, for only by gaining insight into the roots of repetition can it be short-circuited.

Having given in to Socksie's determination to make a place for himself in my world, I bought another cat carrier on the weekend, and when Sunday afternoon came, Connie and I urged him into it. Gallantly willing but intensely frightened by being closed in for the first time in his life, Socksie pressed his face hard against the wire mesh front, turning and turning and turning to keep us in sight but making no outcry. He was a gutsy cat. Having made his bed, he seemed determined to lie in it without fuss.

But as luck would have it, this happened to be a Sunday when we were stopping to have dinner with friends on the way to the city, which meant that it would be closer to five hours than two that the cats would be in their carriers. The ones who were used to the carriers would, we knew, merely curl up and sleep. Would Socksie do the same? We left the back of the station wagon open and moved his carrier out on the flap to catch the breeze—it was an unseasonably warm fall day—hoping that the smell of grass and trees would be reassuring to him.

Three hours later, when our visit was ending and he saw us approaching the car, Socksie released a howl of the purest agony, jamming one of his front paws through a vent and flaring his long claws as though they were the fingers of someone drowning and clutching at the air to save himself. We saw— and smelled—instantly what was the matter. Nervous, frightened, and perhaps simply overdue for relief, Socksie had flooded the carrier. It was awash and he was miserably humiliated. He cried piteously as we held him at arm's length and drained the carrier, lined it with newspaper, and dried his paws with paper towels as best as possible. Still he reeked, as no one knew better than he.

Nor was there much I could do to help him when we got to New York. Had it been one of the other cats, I would have rinsed his paws under the faucet, but there was something intimidating in the square set of Socksie's jaw and his rolling, tough-guy gait. This cat was all gristle and grit, and I assumed that if he felt threatened, he would attack first and think it over later. Leaving it to him to clean himself up, I shut him in the kitchen to get on with the job, which he did and in the morning smelled as fresh and clean as ever.

Aren't cats remarkable? Here was a creature who had lived his life under rubbish, on the edge of a swamp, who had had to make his way over a mud bank to get water to drink, yet the minute he merged himself into a clean and orderly situation, he scoured every bit of himself with a tongue as roughly efficient as a scrub brush until he looked as though he had gone out and bought himself a new coat.

Released from the kitchen in the morning, Socksie explored the apartment, but only cursorily, as though if I and the dog and Kate and Poppy were here, he need not check the atmosphere too carefully. His attention was caught, however, by the view of the street directly below, and he spent wonderstruck hours sitting on a wide windowsill in the living room gazing at the cars and people streaming by on Bleecker Street. But that took only half a day to pall, and he went in search of a place to sleep—more accurately, a body to sleep with. Socksie craved contact, perhaps because he and his siblings, while they were alive, had huddled together for warmth and protection. He tracked down Poppy, but she was squeezed into her niche among the reference books above my desk; no room for him there, so he sought out Kate. She was too old now to restate her opposition to the presence of other cats in her house, but to use her body for a pillow was a liberty she did not permit, as she made acidly clear to Socksie. He granted her the point and settled for a spot on the bed and the use of a pillow for his head, substituting me for both whenever I was not shielded by my desk.

He spent a contented week, giving no indication that he in any way missed the country or his freedom. When Friday evening came, however, Socksie looked from the carrier to me and back again, and it

was as clear as though he had announced it in words
that nothing in the world was going to persuade
him into that carrier, the scene of his mortification,
not force, not food, not his desire to be cooperative,
not while he had breath in his body.

How was I to transport him to the country? If I
carried him in my arms, he would surely bolt when
we hit the noisy street. If I did manage to hold on to
him, he would then be loose in the car and when it
started up, what kind of panic would seize him? At
best, I was going to lose him; at worst, we would
end up in an accident.

It was with dread that I fetched the car from the
garage and parked by a fire hydrant while I ran back
and forth loading the things already in the downstairs hall: suitcase, laundry bag, Hector, Poppy in
her carrier, and Kate, who was hitched to a banister
by her leash. Then I ran up the one flight to get
Socksie.

"Please, Socksie," I prayed as I scooped him up,
"please, please don't claw me." I put one hand under
him, and with my forefinger between his front legs,
locked his legs in as tight a grip as I could manage.
If I had known any wrestling holds, I would have
used those because I feared that if he leaped in a
frenzy from my arms, he would be gone, lost and
quickly killed on the streets of New York. I clamped
him to me and started out.

"Good, Socksie. Good, Socksie," I murmured

soothingly, waiting for the first warning tensing of his body. He was still relaxed as I opened the outside door. I stepped out on the sidewalk. Socksie looked at the people hurrying by with mild interest. A taxi horn blasted. Socksie turned his head slightly to gaze at the source of the noise. I raced to the car. Socksie stepped out of my arms, looked around, chose the bag of laundry and settled himself on it.

And there he rode, dozing, for the whole trip, as quiet, content, and accepting as Kate, who had been riding in cars all her life.

I, who consider myself an all-but-infallible judge of animals' personalities, was wrong at every turn about Socksie. I thought him wild; he was as domestic as a creature can be. I thought him tough; he was gentle. I thought him a fighter; he was placid and loving. I thought him a loner; he was gregarious and, with Poppy, uxorious. The evidence of his benignity mounted daily until finally I recognized that no more sweet-tempered, kind, and affectionate cat ever walked the earth and that his scowling brow came from anxiety, not willfulness.

He was desperately eager to please and became rattled and upset if he was scolded—or even if one of the other cats was spoken to sternly. He tried very hard to do the right thing and often started up in confusion when I entered a room as though I had caught him sharpening his claws on the furniture or sleeping on clean laundry. I recognized his sense of nameless guilt from my own childhood, when I had only to hear a footstep on the stair to hide the book I was reading and look around in panic for what it was I would have been doing had I not been a thoughtless child indifferent to my hardworking mother's health and happiness—or so it was put to me.

Whereas Poppy's infancy left her with an existential anxiety about her worthiness to survive at all, Socksie's anxiety was of the everyday variety: Was he in the way? Was it all right to climb in a lap? Did I like him? Did Connie like him? Did any stranger who came in the house like him? Responsive and receptive, he substantiated the contrarian view I put forth earlier that there can be good effects from a less than ideal childhood. Often enough, in my observation, it creates a sensitive, resourceful, likable adult.

Children who have been subjected to more than the usual number of vicissitudes grow up faster. They learn to solve their own problems, find their own way out of predicaments. They become a quick and accurate judge of people, and they are apt to have a sense of humor because being witty is a protective device, as witness all the comedians who grew up under adverse conditions.

This does not mean that I am in favor of unhappy childhoods, only to say that I think we should not be unduly concerned if we cannot make life completely easy for our children. With fewer material goods, children are likely to be inventive in their play. They learn how things work. They are observant. They learn to conserve, to make do, to be handy at fixing things; they are not too early set in the throwaway ways of consumption and consumerism.

There is a man in my town who owns farms and

acreage as well as commercial properties, and people never refer to how prosperous he is without also adding the bit of gossip that he made it clear to his five children almost from the day they were born that he does not intend to leave his money or property to them. "Not a cent," people say bemusedly. "His children know they are getting nothing." The speakers shake their heads at the idea that a father could be so cruel. But perhaps that father feels, with Hamlet, "I must be cruel only to be kind." He has deprived his children of expectations of inheritance in order *not* to deprive them of initiative, motivation, ambition, the chance and the desire to be the author of their own lives. That he has indeed been kind—and wise—is at least suggested and perhaps proved by the fact that each of his five sons has developed interests of his own; each is established in a life and career that nourishes and supports him. Would they have done as well if they had had "expectations"?

Money, whether in hand or in prospect, has a cushioning effect, a slowing effect, even a dulling effect. You don't have to be alert to opportunity; you can take your time and look around. You don't have to take what you can get, and in making the best of it find that it leads to something quite a bit better. You can afford detours, digressions. If you don't like what you are doing, you can quit and try something that sounds better to you or do nothing at all for a time—or for all time. To have too many options can be paralyzing; when you can do anything, you may do nothing. When every door is open, none may be enticing to go through, and you may end by slouching and schlepping your way through life, achieving little and likely being bored into the bargain.

Entertaining these opinions, I once proposed to write an article entitled "The Disadvantages of Having Money," but no magazine was interested. Editors without exception said that no argument in the world would convince their readers that there were disadvantages to having money, that all their readers wanted to know was how to get hold of more, especially by the painless route of not having to work for it. But I think I am not wrong in praising the uses of adversity. I do not recommend growing up poor, but I am glad I did. Like Socksie, I learned to take care of myself. I do not recommend leaving children to make their way unaided, but I am glad I had to. Like Socksie, I learned to go after what I wanted.

I cannot deny, however, that negative traits can become ingrained along with useful ones. This, too, was true for Socksie. He won a victory over his childhood but not over the lacks in his childhood. Those he was destined to try to fill, refill, and refill again throughout his lifetime. He had searched for love and plenty. He had found them. But nothing was ever enough for him.

No matter that the bowl of crackers was kept full.
No matter that morning and night half a can of cat
food was set before him. He ate, threw up, ate again.
From being a small cat with a big head, he became
a huge cat with a proportionally small head. He
filled out . . . and out . . . and out, and still he ate
until he was as rotund as a small-town banker. Like
the poor boy who becomes a rich man, Socksie could
not recognize when to leave off trying for more. In

that, he was not so much different from this country, which aims to have the gross national product
go up each year even as it becomes ever more clear
that the product of that is national grossness.

It was the same with love. Socksie could be the
length of the house away but a sixth sense let him
know when someone sat down on a chair in the living room. I say someone because it made not the
slightest difference to him if it was Connie or I or a
guest of either sex. If it was all of these—Connie and
I and an assortment of guests—he climbed immediately into the lap of a guest. If one guest was known
to him but another was not, he hastened to the
stranger first. He had to win love from everyone.

Usually the stranger was flattered that this large,
lustrous creature with the build of a marauder but
the disposition of a pussycat had singled him out
and would adjust his lap to make Socksie absolutely
comfortable. If the guest understood cats and
stroked gently behind his ears and under his chin,
Socksie would accelerate his purr to indicate his satisfaction with this attention. But he would not stay.
Ten minutes, fifteen at most, was enough to persuade him that he had won this person. Now he
must move on to the next. And so it would go: from
lap to lap, including Connie's, including mine,
around the circle all the evening.

Alone with him in New York, if my lap was available and another cat arrived at it first, Socksie sur-

veyed the situation, climbed in stages to the top of the chair, put his paws on my shoulder, and let himself down, as inexorable as a mudslide, until he came to rest half-propped against me, half-overflowing onto the cat beneath him. When this cat hitched out from under his weight, Socksie subsided comfortably, contentedly, exactly where he wanted to be. As he grew larger and heavier, his insistence on being close, being held, became something of an ordeal, but Socksie could not do without love. Too much was not enough. Temperance, moderation meant nothing to him. Whereas Bitty had loved out of love, Socksie loved out of need. Bitty went out to people out of security and liking; Socksie went out to people in an endless quest to fill an infillable longing. Bitty was expressing himself; Socksie was trying to complete himself.

I have listened to many a person, almost invariably a woman, express bafflement about why, when they themselves are so loving, they receive so little love in return. They talk about how much they do for other people, how much they give, and how very little comes back to them. Lately it has been a bank teller who has talked about how she stays late to clear up other tellers' overages, weekly bakes her special cream cheese cookies to pass around, drives a colleague's stroke-victim mother to her rehabilitative therapy sessions, loans money to her son that she and he know will never be paid back, and finances nursery school for a grandchild to give her daughter some free time. "And," she weeps, "my children don't even call to ask how I am. The other tellers don't ask me to go out to lunch, and . . ." The litany goes on, always coming down to: "I am so loving. I give so much. Why am I not loved?"

If I thought she wanted to hear it, I could supply the bank teller with three reasons. The first is that self-sacrifice does not win love. It may earn gratitude but not love, and the gratitude is neither deep nor lasting. People quickly pick up on the valuation that your self is worth so little that you are quite willing to sacrifice it to someone else's convenience. Why, then, should they confer love on someone who does not think much of herself? They are more attracted to a robust, self-respecting, free-standing person who can look after herself and pays other people the compliment of assuming they are perfectly capable of managing their lives on their own.

Nor is putting people in your debt any more likely to elicit love. It gives a double-bind message, like ordering someone to behave spontaneously. The minute you are ordered to be spontaneous, whatever you do is, ipso facto, not spontaneous. Just so, you cannot put someone in your debt and then say, "Love me in return," because coerced love is no love at all.

Worst of all is to be needy for love. Nothing is so off-putting. People sense that if they respond, they will be grasped, clung to, perhaps pulled under and swamped because that neediness for love can never be satisfied, because no amount of love poured in will ever fill the emptiness. As was true for Socksie, the asking will go on and on, and no one wants to get trapped in that. It is one thing for a cat to be needy for love, or for a child, because they elicit protective emotions. One is willing, even eager, to be strong and giving because of what Erik Erikson termed the generative drive, that feeling, when you yourself are adult and established and secure, that it is right and rewarding to extend your protection to the small and vulnerable. But when the begging person is an adult, one no more appreciates being solicited for handouts of love than for handouts of cash.

This is not to say that we do not all need love, want love, hug to ourselves a sense of all we might do in life if only we were loved enough. In some buried crevice of ourselves, we even long for perfect love: unearned, unconditional, undemanding, requiring nothing in return and always there to fall back on. But we don't look for it in every person we meet and we don't buy it with pieces of our independence and self-respect. Somewhere we know that our best guarantee of earning love is to be perfectly able to live without it. Or to pretend that that is so. If you are truly needy for love, you must hide the need as though you had leprosy lest people shun you quite as though you had.

I once had a colleague for whom I went out on more limbs than a tall tree possesses. And there was nothing unique about me; everyone who knew Polly did the same. She had a drinking problem, and we shielded her, lied for her, put her in and signed her out of hospitals, covered for her to keep her from being fired. It was true for me, and I would guess for the others as well, that I was a better friend to Polly than to almost anyone else, and I sensed at the time it was because she never asked for help and never expressed any need. She came across as a gallant person, coping to the best of her ability with a problem that was beyond her, self-contained, wryly humorous, absolutely devoid of self-pity. I, and others, pulled Polly out of some horrendous situations and were never thanked, nor did we miss the thanks. If we chose to care about what happened to her, that was up to us. Polly did not seem to need us to. If we chose to value her as a person worth rescuing, that was up to us. Polly did not seem to need us to.

At the time I would have said flatly "did not need us to," no "seem" about it, for it was years before I saw through her wry and patrician manner to the empty, abandoned, fantastically needy core within, so well did Polly hide it, perhaps even from herself, perhaps especially from herself. Had she come on as the hollow reed she actually was, she would never have succeeded in attracting the succession of rescuers who picked her up time and again. We all would have run from the threat of being overwhelmed by such neediness.

• • •

Unless you are a cat, then, I would suggest that no matter how needy you feel for love—or approval or acceptance or support—you never let it show. And even Socksie could have benefited from a sense of limits. Although I grew exceedingly fond of the funny, fat, affectionate, old black cat over the years, I freely and delightedly loved independent Kate and unexacting Chester more.

Trot

Walking into a room of two-legged strangers, I know at a glance which ones I want to get to know. The same is true of four-legged strangers. In both instances, the immediate judgment is based on looks—the attractiveness of a person or animal with a particular type of grace, openness, intelligence, and humor—but on something more than looks as well, something indefinable that used to be called "chemistry" but is more often now referred to as "vibes." Is the attraction chemical? Is it electrical? I can no more explain it than I can explain why pictures come up on a television screen. I only know that there is a recognition across distance of an affinity.

Or, as the case may be, of an antipathy, which is what it was when I first saw Trot. He was sitting on a trash can in an areaway on Perry Street in

Greenwich Village, a cat the color of ashes, looking as comfortable as though he was ensconced on a velvet pillow. When he saw that I was looking at him, he rose up, stretching into an arc, and cried out. He continued to call as I came down the street, and when I drew within several feet of the areaway, he jumped to the sidewalk and hurried to me, rubbing back and forth against my legs so that I had to come to a halt for fear of tripping over him. I leaned down to pet him and he reared up to meet my hands, his cries changing to brays of entreaty.

He was the walking definition of an alley cat, rangy, nondescript, too grimy to be distinguished as gray or white with gray spots, rheumy eyes, and a tail as long as a whip. Close up, he appeared to be a young cat, much younger than I had supposed at first, and not at home in his surroundings. My immediate scenario had been that he was a cellar cat, a cat fed by the janitor of several of the small buildings on the street who allowed him to sleep in one or another basement in return for patrolling the premises for rats and mice. Now I revised my guess, for he was acting like a family cat who had fallen from a window and, unable to distinguish his home building in the welter of look-alikes, had wandered farther and farther and grown ever more filthy in his search for his people. He was begging me to take pity on him, rubbing back and forth as hard as he could against my legs and speaking in pleading tones.

"I'm sorry for your troubles," I told him, where-upon, hearing my voice, he redoubled his beseech-ing cries. "No, no, I can't take you. I have three cats at home."

All the better, he seemed to say. *I'll be good. I promise not to be any trouble. I'll do whatever you want.*

I had never known a cat to try so hard to ingrati-ate himself. He all but turned inside out in his efforts to persuade me to rescue him from life on the streets. I resisted. As I say, the chemistry was not there. I felt nothing but an abstract sorrow for this cat's lot, not the least impulse to better it, and after a few pats on the head, I wished him better luck with the next person who came along and headed off down the street to keep my dinner date.

The cat hurried after me, weaving between my legs. I had to stop. He pleaded with me. I started. He lifted himself on his hind legs like a prancing horse and wrapped his front paws around my leg. I disengaged myself from his hug. He whipped around and grabbed my back leg. No claws. Just as tight a grip as he could achieve without fingers or thumbs.

"Oh, pussycat," I said, "what am I to do?"

He loosed a cascade of small, soft pleas. Feeling that I had no choice, I capitulated and turned to go back the way I had come. He trotted along beside me. We came to the corner of Bleecker Street. I could not let him cross on his own. I picked him up. A flicker of uneasiness ran through him, as though now that he had achieved what he wanted, he, like a groom on his wedding day, realized the extent of the commitment he was making and debated turning back. But then he settled his length into my arms, wrapped his monkey tail around himself, and considered himself rescued and wedded, so much so that when I arrived at my building and set him down to search for my keys but also with the hope that he would take fright and run, he faced the door, put his nose to the crack, and whipped into the vestibule the instant the door opened. The same thing when I unlocked the inner door, and again when we reached my apartment door. I whisked him into the kitchen, showed him the cracker and water bowls and shut the door on him until such time as I could look him over for signs of illness or infestation.

Fifteen minutes late arriving at the restaurant where I was meeting a friend, I explained that I had been waylaid by a cat who adopted me.

"You mean, a cat you're adopting."

"No, no, it was all his idea. I don't even like him. He's ugly—long and skinny and sly-looking, with coarse fur and a pointy face. I like square-jawed cats with fluffy fur."

"So, why didn't you leave him where you found him?"

I did not have a cogent reason except that it had been like making eye contact with a homeless person. Once you have looked into someone else's eyes, it is very hard to walk on by. You have seen the plight; you have registered it. Are you so far gone in inhumanity that you can simply shrug? Which is why, I suppose, we look through or away from beggars—to avoid the eye contact that involves us.

My beggar had made a start on cleaning himself when I got home that night. His face, which I had thought smog-colored, was beginning to show white on his cheeks, and what I had taken to be darker smudges of dirt over his eyes were now revealed to be swatches of striped, brownish gray fur that looked like nothing so much as tattered tieback curtains, the kind blowing in the breeze at the broken windows of abandoned farmhouses. By the next morning he had started work on his shoulders, which required contortions only a cat as long and lank as he was capable of. Day after day the cat scrubbed himself over, pursuing a speck here, a smutch there, leaving no hair unturned, cleaning and ordering and arranging until the moment when he could step forth and present himself to the world.

Finally, in his own eyes he was resplendent; in mine, he was still unusually homely, a white cat splattered with slag-colored spots as random as though somebody had thrown a paint-filled sponge at him. When Connie saw him, the cindery drapes on his forehead did not put her in mind of abandoned farmhouses but of Victorian parlors, lace curtains, and Dickens's novels. "Pity he's a male," she said. "Otherwise, you could name him Aunt Betsey Trotwood."

"Aunt Betsey called David Copperfield Trot."

"So she did. Well, there you are."

Trot stuck. That is the way with a name—you have to see whether it sticks. If it springs to your lips when you are about to call a cat—or a person, for that matter—then it is the right name. I have often been struck by the prescience of parents in naming their children. How did the parents know, when the baby was a day old, that he would grow up to be a Herbert or that she would grow up to be a Bernadette? It seems astonishing, and yet, almost never do you meet someone whose name does not mesh with his or her personality. Or possibly, if it does not, the person has changed it. My mother as a young girl insisted on changing her name from Agnes to Jane, which did indeed suit her far better, and I knew another woman who changed her name to Mercedes, but from what I never learned because she quite rightly said, "If I tell you, you'll always think of me as 'Mercedes, whose name is really Minniola or Minerva or some such.'"

Trot was more Uriah Heep than David Copperfield, but the short sharpness of the name suited him. His pointed face gave him a crafty look and his behavior was smarmy. Determined to be ingratiating, he dogged my footsteps at every turn and tried to butter me up with interested little cries. In uncatlike fashion, he humbled himself in his efforts to be

liked, but the harder he tried, the less I cared for
him; the more he came to me the more I wanted
him to go away. At every turn, he put me in mind
of a case history I had once read of a troubled marriage. The husband adored his wife and could not
let her walk near him without reaching out to pat
her or pull her into his lap for a kiss and a fondle,
while, for her part, she grew more distant and cold
with every passing day and gave him a wide berth
whenever possible. He was baffled and she was
apologetic. She was sorry for her behavior, she told
the marriage therapist; it made her feel like an
ungrateful wretch when she had such a doting husband. But, she added, the truth was that all his
reaching out to catch her hand or pat her bottom or
kiss her neck made her so nervous she could scream.
What she really wanted was some benign neglect.
She did not want him trying to anticipate her every
move, crowding her, striving incessantly to please
her.

"I try to be the perfect husband," wailed the man.
"What more can I do?"

"Less," said the therapist. "Do less!"

That is what I kept wanting to say to Trot. "Oh,
for heaven's sake, just go off and be a cat and leave
me alone!"

Poppy and Socksie had no such problem with
him. To the easygoing, sybaritic, ever-loving Socksie
who had adopted as his motto, "Oh, how lovely it is
to do nothing and rest afterward," Trot was a wel-

come pillow and hot water bottle, and to Poppy he was another ally to buttress her against people. The three of them often slept in a tangle, with Poppy and Trot becoming particularly devoted to each other, and I was happy for them that Trot, whom I did not like, and Poppy, who did not like me, had made such fast friends.

As time went on, Trot became the best-groomed cat I have ever known. He washed his long, narrow body from gleaming nose to the tip of his long, narrow tail at least once a day and gave it a touch-up every hour or two and immediately following meals

and snacks, even a drink of water. Satisfied with his looks, he left off skulking and began to step out, head held high, paws set down lightly but firmly. Where before he had hoped to be tolerated when he entered a room, now he expected to be admired. Whenever there were guests, he made an entrance. He did not stroll; he did not amble. He advanced into the room with all the confidence of a matador entering the ring. He intended to be noticed, and he was.

"What a handsome cat," people said.

"Oh, do you think so?" I would reply, still believing Trot's curtained forehead, stray spots, and nar-

row length disqualified him. But eventually even I had to concede that grooming and an air of thinking well of himself had triumphed over endowment, an observation that set me to thinking about their importance.

Where before, because I work at home, I had dressed in whatever was handy, now I began to buy well-fitting jeans and good-looking pullovers. I combed my hair and put on lipstick every morning whether or not I was likely to encounter another soul, and like Trot, I soon found I was carrying myself with more assurance. I sat straighter at my desk, and the desk itself became better organized, piles of manuscript neater, pencils sharpened, letters and bills filed in their proper pigeonholes.

The point is often made that dress, or appearance in general, is communication, that by how you look you are communicating to others how you feel about yourself. But I had not realized before that the communication goes two ways: out to others but also inward to the self. Being well put together on the outside is a way of communicating to the self that you are a together person inside. You look capable, attractive, and competent; therefore, you are these things. You do not look sloppy or feeble or inconsequential; therefore, you are not these things. Feeling attractive, not feeble, you stand straighter and carry yourself with more authority, even elegance. Feeling capable, not sloppy, you put order and beauty into your surroundings. Feeling competent, not inconsequential, you forgo procrastination in favor of handling tasks as they arise.

Emerson quoted a lady of his acquaintance who declared that "the sense of being well dressed gives a feeling of inward tranquillity which religion is powerless to bestow." That inward tranquillity, I discovered, can be not merely a rare and some time thing but encouraged to stick around by being at one's best most or all of the time, which is not to say that one becomes a person with every hair in place but that, even when dressed in a bathrobe, the bathrobe is not brown and pilled, with spills of egg yolk on its front, but attractively patterned, neatly sashed, and spotless.

The other night I was invited to meet the houseguests of a couple in the village, two women who had come out from the city for the weekend. One was homely as far as her features were concerned, with an angular chin and hooked nose, but she was strikingly dressed in black and white checks, chunky costume jewelry, and red shoes, and her frizzy hair was cunningly cut in a style contradicting the narrow shape of her head. The other woman had average to good features but no makeup on her sallow skin, too long, too straight, unwashed hair, and clothes the general effect of which was gray goods. Which woman was depressed and which upbeat? Which one had lively interests and which crawled into bed at eight every evening? Which one thought well of herself and which hated her life? No question, is there?

Where the self ends and the world begins, there is skin, and over the skin is a second skin: clothes. They are the point at which the person interfaces with the world. People who have bad skin—acne, wrinkles, blotches, scars, pits, sags—are self-conscious about their looks. A friend tells of encountering Greta Garbo in an antique shop on the Upper East Side of New York; as their eyes met and Garbo realized she had been recognized, her hands flew up to cover the lower part of her face to hide the ravages of time. If we are that concerned about what our first—literal—skin looks like, why are we not equally so about our second skin? As a second skin, clothes are just as much a part of our person and a layer whose attractiveness, harmony, and fit are infinitely more under our control.

A freelance graphics designer married to a computer programmer remarked about the different working habits of herself and her husband. She, when she has a project, may spend days in front of her computer in her nightdress, while he must get neatly dressed each morning before he settles down to work in their home office.

Says she, "I'm too absorbed in the work to care."

He gropes to explain his compulsion. "I don't know, I just feel that my thinking might grow sloppy if I'm dressed sloppily, and I can't afford to be careless. It's like I need boundaries, I need to feel pulled together for the work to go well."

The difference may be temperament or it may be the type of work, but I side with the husband. It is easy to wonder if you are home alone whether it makes any difference whether you have washed your face and whether you are wearing a ripped night-gown and run-over bunny slippers. But I suspect it does matter because it is outward evidence of disrespect for yourself, your work, and your environment. How can you do elegant work when you feel disheveled, blowsy, and disordered? A magazine editor of my acquaintance made tremendous fun of her editor-in-chief because the woman invariably freshened her lipstick before picking up the phone when a man was on the line. It does sound ridiculous, but it is the same idea as dressing well even when the occasion does not particularly call for it: you are not hiding behind your looks but using how you look to strengthen and encourage yourself.

There is a woman who lives down the road from me in a modest house. She works in the video store and her husband drives a school bus, so I would assume their income is limited. But whenever the dog and I are walking by and I see her filling the bird feeder or getting her mail from the rural delivery box, she is wearing makeup and is dressed in becoming clothes. "There," I say to myself, "is a woman who thinks well of herself."

Clothes are as revealing as a Rorschach test, and for the same reason. They are a projection of personality. They say what you as an individual are. When it is important to suppress individuality, authority decrees that all must dress alike, e.g., nuns, soldiers. A friend of mine wears Peter Pan collars, an outer expression of her inner feeling of being not quite grown up. Another dresses consistently in black, now and again switching off to white, and she is indeed a person obsessed with facts who sees the world in strict terms of black and white. I recently had occasion to write about a man whose way of characterizing someone he considered lazy or no good was to say, "He walks around in turned-over shoes," and that really does sum up in a phrase the person who takes no pride in himself.

These days many people believe it is unimportant, uncomfortable, and outmoded to dress well, and grant themselves the freedom to wear any old thing no matter the occasion. But the greater freedom, it seems to me, is to dress appropriately for the occasion because then you are free of any concern about how you look. Recently, at a holiday open house, friends who attended in the combat boots and fluttering rags of the liberated were in agonies of self-consciousness and did not at all enjoy the party because they knew themselves to be such standouts in the crowd—and not in a good sense.

At the same party was a woman wearing an eggshell-colored, two-piece silk dress. The overblouse was straight from shoulder to hip, and the short skirt under it was pleated. The neckline was scarfed, with one end of the scarf tossed casually over her shoulder. Her bobbed hair lay close to her head in grooved waves. All that was missing was a foot-long black cigarette holder to complete the picture of a woman out of the 1920's. But it worked. This woman had the face, figure, and hairstyle of a flapper. The style was infinitely becoming to her and she had the courage to go with it, wisely ignoring fashion in favor of what worked for her. Finding what sets you off, what plays to your strong points, what suits you and gives you a lift to wear, what makes you feel full of grace, this is the essence of dressing well.

While clothes are expressing how you feel about yourself, they are also revealing your attitude toward your hosts. The woman in her creamy silk sheath did honor to herself and to her hosts. That she had troubled to look her best acknowledged the trouble the hosts had taken to provide the occasion.

At the other end of the spectrum, I have a friend who comes to visit and the first thing she says as she steps out of the car is some variation of: "If I'd stopped to dress, I'd have been even later than I am," or, "It was raining so I didn't want to wear good clothes," or, "I was just too tired to change, and I knew you wouldn't mind." I do mind. I pick up the passive-aggressive message in the way she dresses, the indication, however unconscious it may be, that, "I'm not going to admit you're important enough for me to take any trouble for," and I am a little hurt, a little angry.

A character in William Styron's *Sophie's Choice* comments: "Dress is important. It's part of being human. It might as well be a thing of beauty, something you take real pleasure in doing. And maybe in the process, give other people pleasure. Though that's secondary." Secondary, perhaps, but still very real, and it is to be remembered that pain can be given as well as pleasure.

Dressed in fur so polished that the tip of each hair sparkled when he passed through a beam of sunshine, Trot carried himself with the grace of a snow leopard and the confidence of Barbra Streisand and wore a habitual expression of hauteur. Did he consider himself a finer fellow than the other cats? Undoubtedly. Was his passion for ladders linked to this? Perhaps, for he loved to place himself above the crowd. A stepladder set up was an immediate invitation to him to climb it. It made no difference if I was already on the ladder and wielding a noisy hedge clipper or messy paintbrush. He pushed past me and draped his long self across the top step.

Yelling only caused him to blink his eyes in disbelief that I could possibly mean for him to get off, and if I attempted to push him off, he embraced the step, hunkered down, and made himself as difficult to pry loose as an embedded tick.

One day I dragged out the aluminum extension ladder, braced it against the house, and climbed to a flat roof at the second-story level to paint some window frames. When I heard strange noises on the ladder, I went to the edge of the roof and peered down. There was Trot slowly making his way up, undaunted by the presence of rungs rather than steps. Using his front legs like arms to hook over the rungs, rung by rung he hauled himself aloft. It took prolonged maneuvering to get himself past the overhang of the roof, but Trot was nothing if not determined and he managed it. With what gave every indication of being a grunt of satisfaction, he swung himself onto the roof, chose a spot on the very edge, and settled himself, a lion on high. That day he was indeed king of the mountain.

That was the thing about Trot. After having succeeded in creating the illusion that he was a handsome cat, he fell into the trap of arrogance. He demanded acknowledgment of the fact that he was not just a fine fellow but the finest of fellows, that he was the incomparable cat.

When Poppy offered to wash Socksie's head, Trot thrust his head between them. When Socksie had himself arranged to his utmost comfort, Trot lay down with his back against him and pushed—a little, a little, a little until he had usurped Socksie's spot. If Socksie cradled his head snugly in the curve of Poppy's body, Trot flicked his thirteen-inch tail absentmindedly, quite as though his thoughts were somewhere else, until he had so agitated Socksie's whiskers that Socksie had to give up his pillow and roll away, allowing Trot, again absentmindedly, to roll into his place.

Poppy gladly accepted Trot at his own lordly estimate and Socksie was too content with life and too laid back to give him any argument. But Trot could not persuade the other cats to acknowledge his specialness. Chester, with his need for distance, moved off when Trot tried to butter him up. Bad-tempered Pickles hissed when he approached and boxed him if he paraded across her path. Kate took no notice of him, and Sweet William, when he came as a kitten, ignored Trot in favor of Socksie, whom he loved and imitated.

Trot had no better success with human beings. Ordinarily it would be flattering to be followed everywhere because it is unusual behavior for a cat, but I did not relish it, nor did I confuse Trot's attentiveness with devotion. He so pussyfooted around that I had the sense of being spied on. He appeared where I did not expect him, materialized in closets, behind doors, under bushes, and the minute he saw that I knew he was there, he rushed to rub against my legs in his smarmy way. His biggest frustration was that he, like the other cats, was forbidden entrance to the henhouse because I refused to have cat hairs in my keyboard. Banging the door by throwing himself at it, he miaowed petulantly to be let in at such volume and for such a long time that I was sometimes tempted to lean out the second-story window and dump a glass of water on his head. When his "open sesame" vocalizations failed to work, he went around to a side window and peered in, on the lookout for any movement inside, and if he detected the slightest, his cries to be let in started up again. Suffering from the minor evil of inflated self-regard, Trot was that most unappealing of combinations: arrogant and humble. It was as though he were saying: "Poor little me, why do you not notice how great I am? Why do you not prize me above all others?"

The fact that I clearly did not, and that, except for Poppy, the other cats did not, ultimately seemed to make Trot a little desperate. If he could not win pride of place, he apparently decided that he would lay claim to the place. He began marking territory as his by spraying. He had been stalking around saying, "This is me." Now he stalked around saying, "This is mine." Supposedly he was a neutered cat, but he had retained the capability of spraying, and now he was making use of it, backing up against a piece of furniture—most notably, one arm of the living room couch—and setting his ramrod-stiff tail to quivering.

When we caught on to the fact that Trot was spraying, we hustled him off to the veterinarian's office. Could she have been mistaken about his being a neutered cat? No, she told us, it does happen that some male cats continue to spray. To put an end to it, we could try hormone pills, which we did, along with scolding, yells, and a smart swat whenever we caught Trot in the act. Nothing worked. Trot was determined to make the territory his, and in trying to have everything, he lost it all.

We packed him off to a horse farm deep in the countryside to be a barn cat, with Poppy to keep him company. We hoped that the two of them would support and sustain each other, but Poppy, bedeviled as always by a thousand fears of her own imagining, immediately fled across the fields, and Trot hung around for a few days, then he too disappeared.

Is something better than nothing or nothing better than something? If you cannot change the situation to suit yourself, should you change yourself to suit the situation? If you cannot have what you want, should you settle for what you have? These are questions very likely to come up more than once in a lifetime, and the answer is not necessarily the same each time.

Sweet William

I doubt that a cat ever asks himself if life is worth living. He simply accepts the goodness of being alive and sets about living with all the curiosity and comfort and convenience he can muster for himself.

Sweet William is as accomplished at this as any cat I know. The only cat I ever bought, he is a snow white longhair, not a purebred, I don't suppose, since I paid only twenty-five dollars for him, but thunderously beautiful and with a disposition an angel might envy. I did not know he was white before I went to see about acquiring him; if I had, I might not have gone because I have never cared for white cats, any more than I care for white cars or white rooms, finding them lacking in distinction. But the vet who called said only that an antique shop in Mountainville had three longhairs for sale.

She, the vet, knew I had lost Kate, my tortoiseshell Persian, some months before and had been on the lookout for something comparably handsome ever since.

To my eyes, all cats are captivating provided their faces are not sharply pointed or their markings disagreeable, as Trot's were, but I am particularly susceptible to the looks of Persians with their broad heads, short legs, cobby bodies, and luxuriant fur. I get the same aesthetic enjoyment from such a creature curled on my living room couch as I do from the painting hanging above the couch. This does not stop me, as is evident, from taking in strays with not much in the way of looks to recommend them, but it is lovely to have at least one real beauty among them. At the moment I am lucky enough to have two, Sweet William and not another cat but the dog, Charlie. Adopted from the Humane Society as a sweet little black and white, roly-poly puppy, Charlie grew—and grew and grew—into a seventy-pound dog with perfect lines, the proud head of a setter, the silky, slightly wavy fur and plumed tail of a golden retriever, and the colors of a border collie. I have never been able to make more of his ancestry than that, but whatever the conjunction of lines, the result is flawless. By caring so much about beauty, I open myself to a charge of elitism, but I cannot deny the pleasure it gives me to have my eyes rest on harmony and elegance.

•   •   •

The three kittens at the antique shop looked as though the proprietor had split open an eiderdown pillow and emptied it into a wicker basket, so white and soft and weightless were they. Whether or not I liked white cats immediately became irrelevant; the kittens were irresistible. The only question was which one I should choose. The proprietor, saying this one was her favorite, plucked the topmost kitten from the heap and held it up to her cheek. "He has the sweetest disposition and loves people," she said. I wrote out a check immediately.

I had then Socksie, Poppy, and Trot. The kitten, used to cuddling with the warm bodies of his siblings, elected the big black cat to serve as a substitute, which was fine with Socksie; the more bodies pressed against him the better. Poppy and Trot were jealous of the newcomer but were quickly won over when it became apparent that the kitten possessed the most equable of dispositions. Placid and unruffled, he was seemingly impossible to frighten or anger. I had an ever-growing impression of his goodness, and one day it came to me that his name should be Sweet William, the name of a flower with color the pink of his nose and the white of his fur.

A friend of mine occasionally remarks what a pity it is that there isn't something you can spray on a kitten to keep it from growing into a cat, not that cats aren't marvelous but kittens are such serious fun as they go about their work of learning about the world. They pounce and play, find delicious menace in shadows and detect ghosts behind doors, arch their backs and dance sideways on little cat feet. And suddenly sleep, dropping off wherever they find themselves. Although a kitten will sometimes inch an object on the mantelpiece over the edge and be interested to observe that the object smashes when it hits that hearth, kittens are in general not destructive, not like a puppy, which chews shoes, slippers, and books, and also not like a puppy in taking endless effort and time to housebreak. Kittens housebreak themselves, although Sweet William was something of a rogue in that respect. He knew where the litter box was and he knew what it was for, but he did not like to use it. This was not a problem in the country where he had all of the outdoors to choose from, but it made life difficult in the city. I asked the advice of a woman exceedingly knowledgeable about cats and she told me this was sometimes a problem in longhairs, as though a gene is missing or gone awry, and, indeed, I had this impression of Sweet William. To be defiant or obstinate or unruly was at odds with his nature. He had no wish to be disobedient; he simply was absent the wish to use a litter box.

In every other way, he was completely lovable. In fact, he was so easygoing and good-humored and affectionate that I found it impossible to judge whether or not he was intelligent. What I finally decided was that he was intelligent enough for his own purposes. He was quick to intuit things that mattered to him, like the living room door being open or the presence of a chicken in a bag of groceries. When the living room was unoccupied, the cats were forbidden access to it so that they would not get cat hairs on the furniture, which made the living room their favorite place to be and the easy chairs their favorite place to sleep. Not just Sweet William but all of them would sneak in if the door was open so much as a crack. There is no lure to a cat like the lure of the forbidden.

As for chicken, the innards in the paper package and the bloody scrapings from the cavity were the food Sweet William was far and away the fondest of, and he magically materialized in the kitchen whenever a chicken was being unwrapped. Too polite to howl, and, in any event, without much of a voice, he made his presence known by standing on tiptoe beside me, leaning against the cabinet and stretching as high as he could, not reaching for the food but reaching to let me know he was there. Unfortunately, I could never give him as much as he wanted because more than a few bites made him sick.

Another of his wishes was to sit in my lap—not really in my lap but held in my arms so that he could bury his face in the crook of my elbow. If it happened that Connie was sitting in my customary place and I in hers, it seemed to baffle Will. Should he get in the right chair with the wrong person or the wrong chair with the right person? If he decided on the right chair, Connie tried to make him comfortable in the particular way he liked of being held quite tightly as a small package curled back on himself, but he knew perfectly well that he was in the arms of the wrong person and after a few moments he moved on to try the other person despite its being the wrong chair.

Even after Connie came to GoWell to live, her cats continued to consider that she was their person and my cats that I was theirs. Chester and Pickles emphatically were Connie's, although Chester, with time, enlarged his loyalties. Sweet William, Bitty, and Kate were mine. Poppy was nobody's, Trot was anybody's, and Socksie related to us both impartially.

If Sweet William had a passion, it was to be outside on moonlit nights, which concerned me because his whiteness made him as visible as though he moved in a spotlight. I was afraid, especially when he was little, that an owl would snatch him up and away in its talons or that a raccoon would consider him fair game. Despite Sweet William's placidity, I knew that this cat would fight a raccoon rather than run, for his lack of anxiety made him fearless, and I did not think he would be able to best a wild animal with its fiercer nature and reddened tooth and claw. Fortunately, so far as I know, Sweet William has never been put to the test, and he continues to sally forth at night, sometimes to sit on the porch and watch the geese fly across the face of the moon, sometimes to prowl through the dark in search of prey. Here again I would have thought his snow-whiteness would be a disadvantage, allowing the mice moving through the grasses to see him coming, but on many nights when he was the only cat out, there would be a mouse offering laid neatly on the altar of the front steps in the morning.

It pained me to see his trophies. I never picked up a dead mouse by the tail to dispose of it without being moved by its perfection: the five tiny toes on each foot, the stiff, sensible whiskers, the paper-thin round ears, the fur softer than velvet in a warm shade of gray. The only unattractive feature of a mouse is its hairless tail, and even that is not nearly so ugly as a rat's tail, which is stiff and thick and unsupple. Once or twice the cats caught a small rat, I suppose because of the proximity of the river, and all I felt as I shoveled the dead body up was revulsion, but I sorrowed a little for the mice.

My tenderness is only in force, however, when the mouse is dead. Live mice frighten me, and I have been known to whoop in the silliest possible fashion when one jumps out of a basket in the toolshed. There was one exception, however. I reached for an old sheet used to collect leaves in, and as I tugged it free of the peg it was hanging on, a mouse leaped from it to a ledge. At the same time, a nest made of leaves and lint fell to the floor. In the nest were four pink hairless newborn mice the size of the first joint of my little finger. I retreated to the door of the toolshed. The mother peeped from behind a can on the ledge, surveyed the situation, eyed me, then ran down the handle of a rake, around and under tools, the lawn mower, buckets and baskets, reached the babies, and gently seized one in her mouth. Scurrying over the cinders flooring the shed, she plunged into a tunnel that dipped under the back wall and disappeared into the mammoth pile of weeds and clippings composting behind the shed. I waited. In a moment she reappeared. Again her bright black eyes estimated the chances of my making a move against her. Her instinct to save her babies won out. She dodged from cover to cover like a soldier under fire, made a dash in the open to the nest, caught up another infant, and raced for the tunnel. Twice more she returned until she had spirited all her infants away. I was aware that I would curse those babies when, grown, they chewed through a box of grass seed and I picked the box up and the seed rained out. Perhaps it would have made more sense to dispose of them now rather than later to set traps for them. But no. They deserved to know the joys of being alive before we played out our predestined roles, and—who knows?—one or more might be smart enough to avoid my traps and lead a long, happy life. A useful life? I have no idea. One hears about the good that worms do, and bees and butterflies, but I have never heard of a positive contribution from mice.

Of all the cats, Sweet William proved to be the one without an agenda. He seemed to believe in ordinary happiness and that things were as they were. He did not try to make life go according to his wishes; he accepted the way it went. Whatever came to him in the way of attention, admiration, comfort, or food, he enjoyed, but he did not force his pleasures or assume they were his by right.

What might account for Sweet William's equanimity? Was he born with perfect chemistry, not a bit too much or too little of this hormone, that neurotransmitter, his nerves well sheathed and in a steady state, his reflexes no more than sensibly active? As someone with a startle reflex that would do credit to a flock of sparrows, I could wish I had been so fortunate. Instead, through the years I have had to search for paths that lead into clearings of repose.

Early in life, in an attempt to get help with the young person's puzzle of who am I, why do I feel this way, what makes me behave this way, I had years of psychoanalysis when that approach to problems in living was at its height of acceptance. I emerged from it so much wiser about myself that I despaired. I had been analyzed—taken apart, shown the roots of my anxieties, given a searing exposure to my fears and inadequacies—and when the dissection was over, I was at a loss how to reassemble the pieces. It was rather like having a watch that works but has a tendency to gain or lose time and taking it to a jeweler and having him say: "Ah, yes, let me show you why this watch of yours doesn't always function as well as it might. You see this little wheel here, and this little pin here? This place where something put a bit of a dent in? Here where a little water got in the works? This spring that is wound too tight?" And when he has dismantled the whole thing, the jeweler turns away with a wave of his hand, "There, now that I've shown you where the problems are, I leave it to you to put the watch back together."

Not for a minute do I mean to denigrate insight. It is invaluable, for without it, one cannot make necessary revisions in the story one tells oneself about the world and how it works. But often a useful amount of insight can be gained without dismantling the whole personality by means of the briefer, more interventionist therapies and approaches that place at least as much emphasis on what is right about the person as on what is wrong.

At the time I am writing of, however, brief therapies were not respectable, so there I was, after four years of the long form, trying to fit the thousand pieces of the jigsaw puzzle back together into a coherent self. One day while at my job at the publishing firm specializing in medical texts, I was given the English translation of a German book to edit. The book, *Autogenic Training* by E. G. Luthe, was based on the work of a psychiatrist named Schultz who used hypnotism in his work. Schultz had discovered that people who could not be hypnotized nevertheless rather easily entered a prehypnotic state in which they were relaxed and open to suggestion, and furthermore that they could readily induce this state in themselves at home twice a day and give themselves the suggestions, thereby reducing their anxieties and increasing their comfort level in the world.

As I began to edit the book, I was scornful that a lifting of depression or a reduction in anxiety could come from lying down with a pillow under one's head and another under one's knees and intoning silently while visualizing one's arm: "My right arm is growing heavy. My right arm is growing heavy. My left arm is growing heavy. My left arm is growing heavy." And then doing the same with each leg. Then starting over with, "My right arm is growing warm. My right arm is growing warm," etc. And after that round: "My forehead is growing cool," and on to, "It breathes me."

"It breathes me is not English," I complained to my boss. "But it's all through the book that way, and the author seems to mean it to be something happening to the person, not something he is making happen."

"Leave it," said my boss, and so I did, grumbling about how stupidly it read and how repetitive it was as the incantations were repeated on page after page. Seated at my desk, legs stretched out and my left arm lying on the desk, I worked on the manuscript, and as the day wore on, I became aware that my left arm was, in truth, heavy and that my legs were heavy and that I felt contentedly relaxed all over, an uncharacteristic way for me to arrive at the end of the day.

I was going out to dinner that evening but I had an hour at home before it would be time to change, and I decided to try what still struck me as a laughably naive approach to neurotic problems. I placed the pillows, lay down, began intoning to myself, "My right arm is heavy," while putting my mind in my arm, that is, sensing it from shoulder to elbow to wrist to fingertips. I went dutifully through both arms and both legs, and then started over, this time with warmth, that is, "My right arm is warm." In the midst of repeating this silently and visualizing my arm, suddenly every capillary in my arm released and my arm and hand were flooded with warmth.

The same warm blush washed over my other arm and both legs, and I sank into a state of tranquillity, as free of tension as an old sock on the closet floor. Although not outwardly high-strung, I characteristically felt tuned to too high a pitch inside, so this state was heavenly to experience. But what really made a believer out of me was that the calm did not disappear when I went out to dinner. I stayed relaxed inside, as light, lilting, and unstrained as Patsy Cline's singing, as comfortable in my body as a cat is in his.

Nothing lasts, of course, particularly good resolutions like practicing autogenic training every day, but I did stay faithful to it for quite a long time and returned to it when I felt edgy or had had a difficult day or needed for any reason to unwind. After a time I discovered that in this prehypnotic state I could experience music as though I existed in a bowl of sound, as though the separation between me and the music had ceased to exist. I was in the music and the music was in me. My liking is for concertos, the symphonic form in which one instrument stands out in bold relief against all the others—I have always found the individual more interesting than the crowd—and I would put on the Bruch Violin Concerto or the Beethoven Fourth Piano Concerto and grow lost to myself in a surround of sound.

The music was an unorthodox addition to autogenic training but I liked it precisely because it did let me become lost to myself, because it cut the flow of unbidden thought coursing through my mind. Since that time of first encountering what is, in essence, a form of meditation, I have tried other types, including TM and various Zen approaches, and my problem is always the same: I cannot stop thinking. Even following Lawrence LeShan's instructions in his book *How to Meditate*, and starting with the simplest way of concentrating on the breath, counting four exhalations and then starting over, I cannot keep myself from pursuing a fancy down the side streets of thought. I drag myself back, but by the count of three, I am off on a new chase. All the guidelines say: *Don't try. Don't struggle. Don't scold yourself. Gently return your mind to your breath. Let the thoughts pass away.* All very well, and I am filled with admiration for the meditators who can sit cross-legged for an hour with empty minds, but I have to provide my mind with a bone to chew on to keep it from straying. For a long time it was music. Then I discovered guided meditation.

A friend made a four-day workshop in Silva Mind Control sound so worthwhile that I signed up for a long weekend. The technique of what the Silva Method calls "going to an alpha level" is not the same as "warm and heavy," but the result is similar in that you are relaxed and withdrawn from the world. In this state, the workshop leader suggests that you picture yourself in a place of peace, which for me is resting on an air mattress in a calm ocean and being gently rocked by the swells. This deepens one's state of relaxation and the leader can then suggest various imaginings, leaving all specifics to one's own vision. For instance, the leader suggests that you are walking on a path and meet an animal and the animal speaks to you, but it is your imagination that makes the path winding or rocky or steep, that has it crossing a field of tall grasses or clinging to the side of a mountain or leading into a jungle; that conjures up a rescuing St. Bernard or a snake or a lion; that hears the animal say it intends to eat you or poison you or lead you to safety. With openness to this free use of the imagination, one can learn an astonishing amount about oneself and what goes on beneath the level of consciousness, and it is far more fun than dragging one's attention back to one's breath again and again.

It was on that Silva Mind Control weekend that I took the first of many repeated journeys to a place that I can see with as much vividness and detail as any actual place I have ever been. After I enter a state of relaxation, the journey begins in an amusement park where I step into a boat to travel through the Tunnel of Love. The boat lightly bumps along the wooden sides of the channel as it enters the tunnel and glides along in darkness. As the boat rounds a blind curve, a scene set into the wall of the tunnel lights up. It is a scene from my life. My father is in the background. My mother is weeping. A small child is trying to comfort her. I recognize the child's smocked dress; my favorite aunt made it for me. I see the scene as a stranger would, see myself in it, and perhaps see it now from an angle different from the interpretation I have given it in the past.

The boat drifts on. More darkness. Another turn in the tunnel. A different scene lights up. This one has not yet taken place, but I recognize the players. I see myself looking angry. I am turning. I am walking out. *So*, I say to myself, *so this is what I am going to do. I am going to slam the door behind me.* A part of me has known that this is how it will end. Now I know it consciously and my courage to take the necessary steps is firmed up.

The boat slides out of the tunnel into sunlight. I step out and descend flight after flight of brilliantly white marble steps to formal gardens stretching to a horizon line of stately pines. I walk along graveled paths past banks of rhododendrons, waves of tulips, masses of pink kolkwitzia, beds of roses, all backed by every shade of leafy green, from the green that is almost yellow through the pure to the green that is almost blue. I come to a pond and kneel and slide my hands into the water. A golden carp approaches and rests on my palms. I murmur, "I hold you with open hands." I rise and go on and come to a white marble temple gleaming in the sunshine. It has no sides, only columns, and in the long slanted shade of one of the columns two people are stretched out in Jamaican planters' chairs comfortably talking, cool drinks at their elbows. I greet Virginia Woolf and Sigmund Freud and join them, telling them what has happened since last I was here and listening to their quiet comments and advice.

I set down this journey with some hesitation, not only because it is my private world but because, in my enthusiasm for the Silva Mind Control experience when it was new, I described this trip to a friend and he laughed and said, "What have you been smoking?" He found it hard to believe that one can trip on nothing but imagination while at the same time having both oars in the water in ordinary life. But it is true, and the inner journey enhances ordinary life, enabling it to be lived more wisely and richly and consciously.

Meditation, any way it is practiced, whether, by emptying the mind or sending it on a fanciful journey or parking it in a place of peace, stills the mind, the yatata, yatata, yatata that goes on incessantly when the brain is not actively concentrating on a task. The unoccupied mind is like a squirrel sitting on a tree branch chattering away to itself, and what the mind is chattering about is the self. We are constantly engaged in telling ourselves what we are like and what the world is like, in this fashion maintaining the world and the self with little or no change. We go on behaving as we have always behaved because we tell ourselves that it is the right way to behave (or the only possible or justified or sensible way). We go on being the person we have always been because we tell ourselves that that is the person we are. We make the same type of choices over and over because we provide ourselves with the same information over and over, arrange to receive the same messages over and over. We justify ourselves and distort the world with our internal monologue. When the monologue reaches closure, the self is off the hook ("I was right to act the way I did. There was nothing else I could do") and the world is on the hook ("Things never go right for me. I never get what I deserve").

A mind other minds cannot easily fool is readily and constantly fooled by itself because our thinking validates our thoughts. If we are to see things more as they are and less as we are, we have to halt the internal dialogue, interrupt the tape loop, break into the closed-circuit TV. This is what meditation does. It stills the rationalizations and the justifications of the self so we can know a bit more about who and what that self is and become as comfortable with it as a cat with the equable disposition of Sweet William.

Sweet William, unlike the usual cat, enjoys accompanying a person on a walk. Most mornings when I set out with Charlie before breakfast to follow our circle route of half a mile down the river road and half a mile back on the old railroad right-of-way, Sweet William pads along behind, walking so lightfootedly that he looks as though he has little springs in his paws. Charlie runs free in the fields, but Sweet William sticks to the road, only getting off it when he hears a car coming. He detects the sound of a car before I do and hastens, although with dignity, into the tall grass, hiding himself thoroughly until the car has passed. This sometimes causes him to fall far behind, but in that case he takes a shortcut he has worked out through a patch of woods and is waiting for us on the right-of-way when we turn into it.

One morning he was a few feet behind me and Charlie was ahead of us, ranging in and out of trees and thickets on the riverbank and wading in the river. Suddenly, without warning, three deer exploded out of the thicket beside me, so close that I felt their hot breath on my shoulder. Eyes blank with fear, they charged across the road, Charlie in pursuit, and went crashing through the woods. My first thought was for Sweet William. Had he been trampled? I called. I plunged into the thicket. I slid around in mud on the riverbank. I scrambled back to the road. There he sat, calmly straightening out the rumpled fur on his back where one of the deer had evidently grazed him.

Sweet William makes no fuss about being small and vulnerable. He makes no fuss about being a cat. At times when another cat would feel threatened, he does not arch his back or hiss or whip his tail back and forth menacingly; at most, he jumps to a higher spot. Dogs are all right with him; he occasionally lies down between Charlie's front paws and makes no objection when Charlie slings a paw over him. Other cats are all right with him; he makes no objection when they pillow their heads on him or nudge him away from his food bowl. People are all right with him; anyone, stranger or friend, can pick him up and hold him. He has a talent for accepting the world as he finds it and himself as he is. Perhaps that is one of the traits Mr. Van Vechten was thinking of when he said that man would do well to emulate cats.

I often come upon Sweet William sitting meditatively, his gaze turned inward, his whole being at peace. How much does his serene disposition, his calm and affectionate acceptance of circumstances and people, owe to such centering? I have no way of knowing. But I do believe this. We, too, need to take the time to sit with ourselves, to put ourselves in touch with the self having this life in this time in this place. Otherwise, life will be what happened when our attention was elsewhere, and we will arrive at the end of it suspecting we have not really been the person we might have been or lived the life we might have had.

Kate

The first cat I had, Robert, was foisted on me by an acquaintance who was moving with her small son to Philadelphia. I would not have acquired him by choice because he was a spindle-shanked cat with a frantic nature, the consequence of living with a hyperactive little boy. He scratched and bit, prowled ceaselessly, sharpened his claws on my legs, and swung on the curtains. On the third day after his advent and at a time when I was radically repenting having agreed to give him a home, the cat in his heedless rush about the apartment dashed out on a tiny terrace and straight through a missing picket in the fence surrounding it. Like a cartoon cat, his legs kept working as he sailed through the air and landed three stories down. He hit the ground running, cleared a high board fence, and disappeared into an inaccessible maze of backyards in the center of the city block. Hail and farewell to Robert, I said, and heaved a sigh of relief that I was rid of the trouble-some creature.

Three nights later, in the ice-cold January dark, I ran out to the corner deli for a quart of milk, and on my way down the block a cat sitting on a garbage can miaowed. I peered at it in the fractured light of a street lamp. It was my sinner. "You survived, did you? Well, just keep on surviving because you had your chance."

I crossed the street on my way back, but he spot-ted me and jumped down and came running. He skinnied through the downstairs door, took the stairs three and four at a time, and when I unlocked the apartment door, hurried in and leaped on the sink, desperate for a drink. Dirty, disheveled, and starving, he was a cat who had come up against life in the streets, and like an atheist in a foxhole, he must have gotten religion, for he was transformed from that moment on. He became the epitome of a well-behaved, sober and obliging, dignified cat, so dignified that I bought him a clip-on bow tie that he wore on his collar and washed carefully each time he ate.

With age and weight and a cat's studious groom-ing, Robert became passingly good-looking, but he always had a skinny, bony tail, and when he died of a pancreatic tumor, what I wanted to replace him was a longhair with a plume of a tail. I canvassed every animal shelter in the city and, even though I was poor then, some of the expensive catteries, but no cat I saw appealed to me. My Aunt Bird, who lived down on the Jersey shore and knew of my search, invited me for dinner one Sunday and suggested we see what the local animal shelter had to offer.

We traveled down the rows of cages, looking at every color, age, and shape of cat but again without my feeling drawn to any particular one. Coming to the end, we exited through a side door, and there, in a cage off by itself, were a half-grown cat and a yarn ball of a kitten. The half-grown cat was nothing special, but the kitten . . . !

The kitten's face was divided in the middle, one half the color of coffee ice cream, one half the color of German chocolate cake. The rest of her coat, ranging from lightest blond through rust to richest mahogany, was as varied and subtle as marbleized endpapers in an old and valuable book. I thought she was the loveliest animal I had ever seen—except for her ratty tail.

Could I overlook that? For the sake of that extraordinary, split-color face, I could. I went to the office to inquire if the kitten was available. She was not. The director of the shelter intended to keep her for his own. "Are you sure?" I asked. "Would you just check?" A phone call was placed and the answer came back: if I really wanted that particular kitten and would pay three dollars (this was a while ago), I could have her. I returned to the cage and unlatched the door.

"First, Miss Beautiful, we have to see whether you like me." I lifted the kitten from the cage, expecting a purr to rumble into being. Instead, the kitten pulled her head back and studied my face with a brow as fiercely beetled as an owl's. Just when it seemed that I was not going to pass muster, a small paw came forward and patted my nose.

I paid the three dollars, named her Kate, and on the way home, while she rode nicely relaxed in my lap and I scratched lightly behind her ears, she turned and sank her small, needle-sharp teeth into my hand. No warning. No reason. I was dismayed. Why would the kitten bite the hand that was proposing to feed her for the rest of her life?

It was programmed into her, I soon learned. Never, not once in the twenty years we were together, did Kate unsheath her claws. Not once did she scratch me. But let an action displease her, let her decide she had had enough of whatever it was—petting, combing, nail clipping, examination by the vet—and her teeth would seek the nearest expanse of skin, almost always simply laid on lightly in warning that you were to cease whatever you were doing but very occasionally clamped down in earnest. I scolded. I yelled. I spanked, sometimes with considerable fervor, but nothing broke Kate of this piece of behavior.

Although the single piece of behavior angered me

when it happened, I soon came to love this cat unreservedly. She was more herself than any creature or
person I have ever known. Her spiritedness, her
strong defense of her boundaries, her perfect sense of
who and what she was commanded my respect and
made her seem less a dependent than an equal. I
found her admirable and complicated and infinitely
worth being loved by. An even-tempered cat like
Sweet William is a pleasure to have around, but
with a cat like Kate who has a mind of her own and
will stand toe-to-toe with you, the bond goes deeper and has many turnings.

When I was in college, I had a blind date with a
fellow from Dartmouth who turned out to be, not
just attractive, but brilliant, witty, vivid, sparkling
with ideas that were new to me. I was dazzled. I
spent the evening hanging on his words, agreeing
with every notion he threw out and, in general, acting worshipful. I may even have told him how wonderful I thought he was. That first date was our last;
I never saw him again.

Having been socialized as a female to be self-
effacing and supportive and admiring in the company of a male, I had to grow older and wiser before I
learned that homage quickly palls. What holds one's
attention is another mind, another personality,
another autonomous being to come up against. A
worthy partner must also be a worthy adversary. A
man worth his salt likes the challenge of an equal. I
read somewhere that the Duchess of Windsor knew

this. The first time the King spoke to her, it was at a luncheon and he politely asked what she as an American thought of England. She replied that she would not have expected the King to ask such a trite question and turned her back on him, which instantly riveted the attention of this man who was used to having people fawn on him and was the beginning of their love story.

On that first day of Kate's advent in my life, the unpleasant surprise of her biting was more than matched by a most pleasant surprise. I was not destined to have another rat-tailed cat after all. Her tail had apparently been soaked by her cagemate's chewing on it in their play, and when it dried, it gave promise of growing into the gorgeous, gently waving plume I had wished for.

When it came time to take the train back to the city, I curled Kate's pretty tail around and tucked her into my coat pocket. She traveled without a cry or whisper, without squirming, with no sign of fear, and this too was to prove utterly characteristic. In uncatlike fashion, Kate was spooked by nothing. No noise, no crowd, no strange place, no moving vehicle panicked her. Her aplomb was unshakeable. As she grew larger, I took to carrying her, facing backward, on my shoulder, supported in the crook of my arm. Riding thus, she went anywhere, through city streets, on trains, to the homes of strangers, all the time merely gazing with interest at the commotion around her. Perhaps, just as she was the most loving of cats because she felt strong enough to fend off any encroachment on her autonomy, so also was she the least timid because she felt perfectly capable of taking care of herself.

Passersby seeing the burnt-sienna colors of her coat, her luxuriant tail, and her extraordinary face frequently asked if she was a raccoon, and when I said she was a cat, they asked what kind. Rather than admitting I did not know, I said she was an Aspacian, coining the term in honor of her acquisition at the ASPCA. People rolled the name so lovingly on their tongues and nodded with all the satisfaction of having added to their store of knowledge that I kept on identifying Kate as that even after I found her look-alike in a cat book and recognized her to be a tortoiseshell Persian.

The second question of passersby was whether they might pet her, and the answer had to be no, that she might possibly bite. It pained me to say this because it made Kate sound vicious when she was actually the most devoted of creatures. But only to me. She was a one-person cat, as dedicatedly so as any dog.

Soon after Kate and I took up together, I saw a play by Samuel Beckett in which a character period-ically popped out of an ashcan to inquire, "Is it time for lovin'?" This became a favorite phrase for Kate and me. When the kitten tired of tumbling about the apartment in pursuit of crackling balls of cello-phane and catnip mice, she stood beside my desk chair and spoke. "Is it time for lovin', Kate?" I would say, picking her up, and she would rumble that indeed it was. "Well, then, kiss me, Kate," I'd say and turn her over and snuffle her tummy with my warm breath, and she would reach up and pat my cheeks with one cream-colored and one choco-late-colored paw.

Just as she did not use her claws as other cats did, so Kate did not purr like other cats but made throaty sounds instead. I recently read this: "Cats can make up to fifty sounds, which, to other felines, form understandable messages with precise meanings." I would add that not only to other felines are the meanings precise but also to the person attuned to the cat. Kate could perfectly order me to open a door or change the litter box or turn on the faucet in the bathroom so she could play with the drip, and she could summon me excitedly to look at a pigeon when one landed on the roof opposite. One time she called and I joined her at the window. "Where, Kate?" I said. "I don't see a pigeon." She looked at me, spoke her sound for pigeon, and then shifted her gaze out again. I followed it, and there, high in the sky, was an airplane. "Right you are, Kate," I agreed. "If it flies, it must be a bird."

Once when I took her on a weekend visit, I was standing in the farmhouse kitchen talking to my hostess when Kate, just emerging from kittenhood, strolled into the room and spoke. "What is it, Kate?" I said absently. "You want to be picked up?" She affirmed this. "Well, then, sit up," I told her, and she perched on her haunches and raised her front legs as a child raises her arms to be picked up. And indeed, "She's just like a two-year-old," my hostess said wonderingly.

About that time I bought my first car, a little red Volkswagen. On the few occasions in which Robert had ridden in a car, he had screamed unrelentingly and I dreaded a repetition of that with Kate. I underestimated the intrepid Kate. As it turned out, she adored traveling. The longer the trip, the better she liked it. On drives to Florida to visit family, she showed a clear preference for Howard Johnson motels, and I wondered if it was because the layout of the room was almost invariably the same. Did she think we drove around all day and returned to the same room every night? In any event, she would walk in the door trailing her leash, use her litter box, have a long drink of water, eat her tuna (I know tuna is bad for cats but Kate would eat no other canned food—it had to be tuna, it had to be Figaro brand, it had to be the large, not the small, can— and she lived to be twenty years old), then settle down in the exact center of an armchair, paws neatly tucked under, and consider herself perfectly at home.

In the morning, after breakfast and such-like, she would return to the chair to watch while I packed. One morning she vanished from the chair and I was a bit panicked until I discovered that she had walked out to the car by herself, jumped in, and was already settled in her usual place on top of a suitcase. After that, I gave up carrying her and simply said, "We're here, Kate," or, "Time to go, Kate," and let her get herself from car to room and back again. If our room assignment happened to be a flight up, I'd direct her to the stairs and she would glide up them, then proceed down the corridor, hesitating at each door as though it were a game of musical chairs, until my insertion of the key indicated that we had come to the right one.

One night in a motel I was awakened by her cries, which sounded oddly remote. I turned on the light and searched the room, all the while talking so that she would answer and I could trace her voice. It seemed to be coming from beneath the floor. Finally I crawled under the bed and discovered a foot-square hole in the boards. "Oh, dear," I thought, "am I going to have to ask the motel owner to tear up the floor?" With my head in the hole, I asked her question after question because a questioning inflection in my voice always prompted her to answer, and then I sang her favorite song. On the eighth chorus, she found her way back through the maze. Her tail brushed my face, and I reached down and pulled her out.

One icy night at a gas station in Virginia, the last inch of her trailing leash was all that stood between me and never seeing Kate again. It was long past our usual stopping time, she was impatient, for she was the only one who had not gotten a pit stop during the day, and when I rolled down the window to pay for the gas, she went out of it. Startled by the lights and the people, she was disappearing over a snow bank into blackness when I launched myself flat out and caught the end of her leash.

That was the only time I knew Kate to panic, and even then she was not bolting, merely moving swiftly to greater safety. I have seen her come nose-to-nose with a horse and merely sit up on her haunches and study this unusual creature. I have seen her lazing on a rock wall and merely flick her tail when a mole surfaced underneath it. I have seen her hanging by her leash out of the window of the car and merely give herself a shake when I returned from inspecting a place we might stay and rescued her.

Kate was dauntless. In her zest for travel and easy adaptation to any circumstance, she reminded me of those redoubtable English ladies of the nineteenth century who went out to the Middle East and joined desert caravans or followed the trade routes to the Far East and got themselves smuggled into Tibet dressed in men's clothing. Such women—and Kate—possessed supreme self-confidence.

There was nothing soft or timid or compromising about Kate. She was drawn in firm, bold strokes, which discouraged anyone, person or animal, from treating her lightly. Hector, the golden retriever, who came when Kate was about four and necessitated trading in the Volkswagen for a station wagon, held her in the utmost respect, although, to my knowledge, she never disciplined him by more than a stern look. The look was enough. I sometimes glanced around when we were traveling to discover the large dog squeezed upright into a corner while Kate luxuriated at full length in the space intended for him. It was not what Kate did that asserted her authority. It was a matter of "presence."

Kate had it. Actors have it, although some to a

more marked degree than others. The great ones walk out on stage and immediately the stage belongs to them; they take possession of the space and command everyone's attention. One assumes that it is something they are born with, but actress Rosemary Harris, in an interview in the *New York Times*, commented that she thought presence was something that could be developed, that it has to do with one's carriage and poise. Laurence Olivier, she said, to give himself presence always came on stage imagining that he was carrying a large green umbrella that caught everyone's attention and pulled their eyes to him, while Julie Harris imagined that she was riding on a pink elephant when she made her entrance.

We are, on the surface at least, the images we project, whether the image is of a vulnerable, hapless, easily dominated person, an angry, defensive person, or a strong, confident person. Why not make the best choice possible? Why not come on carrying a green umbrella or riding a pink elephant to give oneself presence?

For a long time, self-assurance, self-confidence, and self-esteem may be only attitudes, artificially maintained by green umbrellas and pink elephants, but attitudes determine what happens to us. Playwright Lorraine Hansberry said of her father that he "carried his head in such a way that I was quite certain there was nothing he was afraid of."

The resonant voice of a man I know guarantees him attention, while a friend's elegant posture ensures her deference. We speak of a man having a lordly air, a woman behaving in queenly fashion. Who knows what they are experiencing inside? They may be a quivering mass of jelly, but the world sees the lordliness, the queenliness, and responds to the attitude as if it were true, providing feedback that, in turn, bolsters the person in being these things. The assumed becomes the real. Responded to as a person with "presence," the "presence" becomes ever more characteristic of the person.

Kate was always her own self, not my plaything or possession or pet. Since this is true to a greater or lesser extent of all cats, I sometimes think that to live with a cat is a lesson in sharing power. A cat is such an autonomous being that you cannot force your will on it. You have to acknowledge that there are two individuals and they each have a right to their separateness. The relationship of cat and person seems to me a paradigm for marriage, and for friendship as well: two independencies coexisting, affirming and bringing pleasure and support and solace to each other but neither one exerting power or coercing love. In contrast, the relationship between person and dog is, in the main, a model for what a relationship should not be: "I'll take care of you, protect and shelter you, and in return you shall be obedient to my wishes." A dog has a master; a cat has a person. It is not by accident that we speak of dog owners but cat lovers.

But even a cat can be subverted. Polly, whom I described earlier in connection with Socksie, had a cat she called Waifer because when he came to her as a kitten, his enormous eyes in a tiny body made him look like a waif. He grew up to be a brindle cat of preternatural intelligence, and still with those huge eyes, eyes that he kept trained a good deal of the time on Polly. Polly was a binge drinker, sober for weeks and then falling-down drunk for days, and although it might not seem quite credible, Waifer had the same look in his eyes as a child who watches his parent anxiously for signs that the drinking has started or is about to start. As drunk as Polly got, she always managed to open a can of food for Waifer once a day, so it was not that the cat was worried about where his next meal was coming from. He was worried about her. When Polly passed out, he sat close by her head, his eyes on her face, and when one or another of her friends came to boil an egg, which was all she would eat, he met the visitor at the door, miaowing urgently, and ran ahead to lead the way to where Polly lay. There was no mistaking his concern.

It was touching to see this cat's devotion. But it was sad to realize that it made Waifer false to his own being. Independence, self-ness are at the very center of a cat's nature, but Polly undermined Waifer's separateness. She could not have dominated Waifer by her superior strength but she managed it easily through her weakness. She bound him to her through fear, not for himself, but for her, which is often the strongest kind of bondage there is.

We are all aware, I think, of the danger of being subjugated by a stronger personality, but much less alert to how weakness can be used to dominate. Being dictated to is at least clear-cut; ordering oneself around out of compassion or concern or generosity is much more subtle. You lend your strength to hold the other up or see the other through. You try to head off upset or provocation. Anything to keep the peace, to keep the person on an even keel. But what anything turns out to cost is yourself. You have forfeited your right to be yourself.

The motive is love, which is touted as an unmitigated good, but it is not, not when it means subverting your own nature to someone else's ends. What is good is the love of two complete persons, each responsible for the caliber of his or her own life. That is what makes for a fortunate love, and, as Dorothy Sayers rightly remarked, "Love has got to be happy, for fear it should become all-important."

For Waifer, it was unhappy and thus all-important. For Kate, it was happy and she took it for granted like the ground she walked on and the air she breathed. Several times a day she announced it

was time for lovin' and held out her front paws for
me to swing her up and hold her upside down in my
arms so that she could pat my face with her soft
paws. She was the only cat I have known who often,
by preference, lay on her back, propped up among
the pillows on the couch like an odalisque. I teased
her that she did it to air out her Persian pants, and

for all I know that was her reason, since the fur on
her back legs was particularly long and luxuriant.

Like a woman so beautiful that she does not have
to worry whether her hair is combed or her lipstick
is on straight, Kate was careless of her looks. A lick
here, a lick there, and she called the washing-up
done. Whenever I decided that her personal hygiene

had grown a little too casual, I zipped her into a mesh bag and gave her a bath in the kitchen sink, using the spray hose to wet her down and shampooing her through the mesh. She never gave the least sign of minding it. She quite liked water and often curled up in the bathroom sink, finding it just the proper shape to cradle a cat, and dozed there with the faucet dripping on her.

On the proceeds of a book I had written, I bought GoWell, which was then a four-room, tenant farmer's house in such an advanced state of disrepair that the book did not have to be much of a success for me to afford it. A handyman's special if ever there was one, the house was mantled in poison ivy vines so rapacious they had bullied their way into the rooms through the clapboards and pulled the front porch into a dispirited sag. But Kate and Hector and I cared nothing about that because we were in love with the river that ran beside the house. Hector, being a golden retriever and therefore a water dog, swam, waded about in its shallows, and retrieved sticks as often as he could persuade anyone to toss them into the current. Kate was more circumspect, sitting on a favorite rock at the water's edge but letting her gorgeous tail trail in the water. On very hot days, she jumped from rock to rock on the remains of a long-ago dam near the bridge and joined Hector in the middle of the river, where they both stood with their forefeet in the rushing, cooling water. Not often, but sometimes, she would ask to come along with me on the rubber raft, where again she would let her tail float in the water as we drifted on the current. Once we tipped over. By the time I righted myself and reached for her, she was already swimming for shore. With no apparent haste, she climbed out on the bank, gave herself a shake, and strolled away nonchalantly to sit in the sun.

Such was Kate's happy life when, to her way of thinking, disaster struck. This was the advent of Boston, the runt of the four found kittens to whom I gave special treatment. In the beginning, Kate, after taking note of the presence of the basket of kittens, paid them no further attention until three of the kittens went to new homes and only Boston was left. By that time, my experiment in hand-raising

Boston had not only transformed Boston into the brightest, most engaging and affectionate kitten imaginable, but lured me into feeling every bit of the love I was offering him. Kate had always seemed so independent, so self-contained and secure, that I did not think of the effect on her of my delighted interaction with Boston, and I woke up too late to the realization that she had become blindingly jealous of him.

I tried to remedy the situation, but she went stiff with rage when I picked her up. She screamed and growled, hissed and spat—at me, at Boston, at anyone who came near her. Guests were terrified of her, and even I grew afraid to handle her. Never now was it time for lovin', never time to spring into my lap, turn upside down and pat my face with one blond and one brown paw, never time to ride the raft or curl up by my side in bed or come looking for me with glad cries. She grew mean and vicious. One day in New York, riding on my shoulder when I went around to the garage to fetch the car, she bared her teeth and glared at me so wildly that I feared she was about to sink her teeth in my cheek. I snatched her off my shoulder and pinioned her front legs, and when we arrived in the country, she was so beside herself still, growling and hissing, that I threw her in the kitchen sink and turned the cold water faucet on full to bring her to her senses.

Who would have dreamed that an animal could

sorrow so fiercely and so unrelentingly? I understood what Kate was going through because I
remembered a time in my own childhood when I
was about six or seven and we joined a cousin of my
mother and her son, who was my age, at the shore
for a two-week vacation. By the end of it, my parents had fallen in love with the freckle-faced boy and
there was much talk of taking him home to live
with us. Whether the talk was serious or joking I do
not know to this day, but I, an only child, was in
agonies of jealousy. I cannot remember ever being
more miserable—or feeling more isolated and
unwanted. My security was shattered. I cried myself
to sleep night after night.

It was not, then, that I didn't sympathize with
Kate and understand her misery, but I felt helpless
to do anything about it. I was in the position of a
spouse in a secure, loving, satisfying marriage who
suddenly, without in the least willing or wanting it,
falls helplessly in love with someone younger. I did
not want to pull Kate's world down, and with it a
part of mine. I loved and admired her and valued
what we had together. But I could not give up
Boston.

Observing this cat racked by jealousy taught me
nothing except that jealousy is an engulfing, devastating emotion. I felt that I understood the story
of Medea and every other crime of passion in a way
I would never have come to had I not seen Kate

transformed into a virago. But I have no idea of a remedy. It seems to me that jealousy, like a violent storm at sea, cannot be wished away, only ridden out.

The remedy came for Kate ten months after the storm overtook her. I went out to look for Boston one evening at twilight and found him with a half-consumed rabbit. A thousand times after that I wished I had had the wit to realize that such a tiny cat as he was could not have brought down a full-grown rabbit and that the rabbit must have been dying or dead when he came upon it. A little further thought and I would have remembered that a crew had sprayed defoliant on the weeds along the railroad track a few days earlier. But all I did was pick up Boston and tease him about being glassy-eyed and round-bellied from overeating. A day later Boston was dead. When I came back in the house after burying the little body, Kate, for the first time in months, climbed into my lap, turned herself upside down and reached up to pat my face. How did she know her hated rival was gone? She knew, and from that instant on she was her old self. It was time for lovin' again.

So, when the terrible time is over and the rival is out of the way, it is possible to forgive and go on as though it never happened. Kate taught me that at least.

• • •

I sometimes amuse myself with the game of imagining if cats were people what sort of people they would be. I think I can make some pretty accurate guesses about Kate. Aristocratic and autocratic, she would have been an intrepid adventurer on a par, as noted, with Alexandra David-Neel and The Honorable Jane Digby. She was not particularly curious but she was always interested, and she was happy to have the blessings of comfort but unconcerned when it was absent. One of the clearest memories I have is of Kate perched on a broken-springed chair, her coat white with plaster dust, looking on benignly as I demolished old walls at GoWell and broken plaster rained down around her.

She would have been an atheist, I am certain of that, but then so would all cats. Unlike dogs, they are not worshippers. They seem neither to desire nor to need gods. I think she would have been a feminist. I cannot imagine her being an accepting part of what has been termed the "proletariat of house- and office-keepers, husband- and child-servers, sexual gratifiers and ego boosters" that women once were and still often are. She was female through and through but not feminine, not dependent or self-sacrificing or self-effacing. She would have been a strong-minded marcher in a cause, although never a joiner.

If she were an actress, she would have been

Katharine Hepburn; a singer, Maria Callas; a politician, Margaret Thatcher. Like Thatcher, she might have had just a touch of the scold, saying to the country, "Pull up your socks. Enough of this whining about rights, privileges, and entitlements. You have a will. Use it!" She would agree with Italian psychiatrist Roberto Assagioli: "Of course we are conditioned by the past but we have the power to disown it, to walk away, to change ourselves." In short, Kate would say, "Take responsibility for your life. Do it. Get on with it."

Curiously enough, other cats came as the years went by—Poppy, Socksie, Trot, and Connie's Chester and Pickles—and Kate was perfectly agreeable about their presence. She was quite capable of distinguishing my ordinary liking and affection for them from my devoted involvement with Boston. She knew my heart had been captured in a quite different way, and she could not bear it. But with Boston gone, all was as before. We quarreled; we made up. We criticized each other; we admired each other. We made demands; we were generous. We walked away; we came together. We had, in sum, as simple and complex a relationship as between any two strong-minded personages.

She was about fifteen when she fell ill. Ordinarily, I would have picked it up at once, and indeed I was aware that she was not eating, but it was the

Christmas holidays and I was too distracted to do anything about it until suddenly, on New Year's Day, she seemed really ill, so ill that I took her to the emergency room of the Animal Medical Center. A doctor there diagnosed a pyloric tumor and suggested that, because of her age it would be best to put her down rather than operate.

"But not here," I said. "I'd rather have it done by a vet she knows."

On the way home, I remembered her passion for peppermint stick ice cream. Whenever we drove to the country, I stopped at a Howard Johnson's and bought a cone, and Kate licked one side, her pink tongue darting in and out at a furious rate, while I licked the other; when we came close to meeting in the middle, the rest, cone and all, went to Hector. I couldn't find peppermint stick in the city, but I bought some vanilla ice cream, let it melt, and dribbled it into her mouth. She swallowed a bit that day, more the next, much more the next, and on the fourth day switched back to her usual diet of tuna.

She recovered and lived for another five years, until she was twenty, but after her illness she began to grow old. My beautiful Kate slowly became frail and shrunken and tattered, her coat dull and oddly disheveled. She remained as totally herself as ever, but she could no longer jump in my lap; her hind legs had no spring left in them. I would hear a scratching sound, like a mouse scrabbling for a foothold, then her imperious voice.

"What is it, Kate?" I'd say. "Is it time for lovin'?"

All she could do was paw at the leg of the chair where I sat reading and rumble the double tone in her throat that commanded, "Pick me up."

Other times she would call to me from a distance, and I would find her in a corner, turning helplessly from one wall to the other, unable to find her way out. When she stumbled into Hector, the only other being she truly cared about, she scolded him with a hiss for being in her path, and sometimes she seemed unable to remember where her food and water were and I had to carry her to them.

I used to assume that when looks and almost all else that makes the personality remarkably dear are gone, love must go too. But now I know that looks and age have nothing to do with love, that when there has been trust and companionship, you go right on cherishing each other.

There is something else about love that Kate taught me. She lived in a cat world and I live in the human world, and there is a chasm between. But so is there a chasm even between people. "A wonderful fact to reflect upon," wrote Charles Dickens, "that every human creature is constituted to be that profound secret and mystery to every other." Fall in love and you yearn for merger, for two to become one, to live in one and the same world. Be lucky enough to

progress to mature love and you realize that
inevitably you live in separate worlds, in what
Rilke spoke of as "two solitudes." Kate taught me
there is nothing regrettable about that, that it is
possible to accept the individuality of the other—
even to celebrate it—and nevertheless love wholeheartedly across the chasm.

The End

Time has gone by, and different cats live at GoWell now. Bitty, Poppy, Chester, Socksie, Trot, and Kate are gone. Only Sweet William, more beautiful than ever, remains.

Often I have heard people say when they have lost a beloved pet that they will not get another because they become too attached, the pain of loss is too great. I cannot deny the pain. Sorrow was a knife in my heart when I had to accept that Bitty was gone. He dashed out one midnight between the legs of departing guests, just as I speculated he had done a year earlier from a different house. It was far from the first time Bitty had stayed out at night, and although I would have preferred him to be inside, I did not become concerned until the next morning when I opened the front door, expecting that eager little body to come bustling in with cries of greeting, but the porch was empty. I called. I whistled.

"He'll turn up," Connie said.

"Sure," I agreed. But seeds of worry began to sprout, and when I took Charlie for his morning walk, I scanned the thickets and called Bitty's name every few steps. At mid-morning, I left off work and searched the grounds and woods; mid-afternoon I searched the fields opposite the house; late afternoon I searched a horse barn three fields away, the nearest structure and the only one within a conceivable distance for Bitty to travel.

"Perhaps someone thought he was a stray and picked him up," Connie suggested. "He lost his collar a couple of weeks ago, remember?"

"Bitty wouldn't go with anyone else," I said. It was being utterly certain of this that made me fear he was injured or trapped in some way that made it impossible for him to get home. By the second day of his disappearance, I was searching full-time, desperate to find him before it was too late to make him whole and well. By the fourth day what kept me going was the recollection that Pickles, several years before, taken by Connie on vacation to a cabin in the woods in New Hampshire, crawled back to the cabin with a broken leg, broken pelvis, and smashed tail four days after she had gone missing. I imagined Bitty this dreadfully hurt, lying somewhere in the bristly fields or in the woods, too weak to call out, and I could not stop searching.

Maybe just there, in that clump. Maybe in the one just beyond.

After four days I made myself accept that if I found Bitty now, it would only be his body, but I kept on searching, needing the closure of knowing how he had died. Each time I returned to the house, a pinpoint of hope flared that somehow, miraculously, that compact body would pop up on the porch, that merry voice speak. I imagined how fiercely I would snatch him up and say over and over, "Oh, Bitty, I'm so glad, I'm so glad!"

It did not happen. At the end of a week I gave up the search and accepted that one year of pure love was all there was to be. In my notebook I wrote this:

"Dear, dear Bitty, my beloved Bitty, is surely dead. I am desolate. I loved him so wholeheartedly, so unreservedly that I can hardly get past his loss.

"I never failed him, never failed to love him completely. I was always tender, always gentle, always there for him. But this was because he called forth the very best in me with his unfailing good humor, his communicativeness, his pleasure in being loved. He reveled in love, and I had no reason to hold any of mine back, for unlike it might be with a person, he would never make demands I could not or would not want to meet, never exploit or manipulate me, never turn the depth of my feeling to his own ends. I could be utterly unguarded and love without reservation—and I did."

It was three months later that some animal

dragged Bitty's frozen body to the edge of the field across from the house, where I found it and buried it, weeping again as I had wept three months earlier.

Yes, it was scalding to lost Bitty, but if I had protected myself against the pain of losing him, I would have missed out on the joy of loving him. T. H. White, the English author of *The Once and Future King*, had a beloved setter named Brownie, and when she died, he wrote to his friend David Garnett: "Brownie was my life and I am lonely for just such another reservoir for my love. . . . But if I did get such a reservoir it would die in about twelve years and at present I feel I couldn't face that. Do people get used to being bereaved? This is my first time."

Garnett replied: "You ask should you buy another bitch. One can only speak for oneself, but I think the best antidote to the numbing obsession of grief is having responsibility to a living creature. So I would say Yes: you should."

White took his friend's advice and bought another dog, again a setter, saying that it would be foolish to waste all the knowledge Brownie had given him about setters and that, in any event, no setter could ever remind him of Brownie any more than one woman would remind him of another.

No cat ever again reminded me of Bitty, but other strays have come to GoWell and been welcomed— Annie Orphan, Oedipuss, Bumpy, and Zachary.

They have given me a reservoir for my love, which might have dried up within me had I turned them away because I could not face the prospect that one day they, like Bitty, will be lost to me. One does love again, whether it is an animal or a person. The caring is different because the animal is different, the person is different, but it is caring and it needs to be spent. Better the sharpness when loss comes than the drying up of unspent love.

"Do people get used to being bereaved?" White asked. I cannot believe they do, but one does get more used to the idea of death when, because of the shorter lifespan of animals, one has gone through the experience several times. When death comes in the fullness of age, as it did to Kate at twenty, it seems natural and to be welcomed rather than regretted. Kate's stunning coat had thinned and grown dry, her eyes had dimmed, her thoughts were confused, her joints had stiffened. Her body was no longer a good or comfortable place for her to live. It was not sad when the time came for her to move out of it; it was right.

One afternoon I was near her when she let out a cry and began backing up rapidly, as though something was attacking her and she was trying to get away. I imagine that she was trying to escape the blinding headache of a stroke, for in the next moment she fell and even before I reached her she was dead.

I would like to go like that: time only for a sharp cry of surprise and then oblivion. If it does not work out that way, though, I shall remember Socksie and try to meet death with the same dignity he did. I was in the hospital with a ruptured disk in my back the September after Connie joined me in the country, and when she came to see me, she mentioned that Socksie did not seem to be around. Connie was juggling her practice, running the house, feeding the animals, walking the dog, and doing errands for me, so she was not sure when she had seen him last.

"He couldn't be lost," I said. "Socksie loves his comfort too much to go any farther away than the rose garden."

"Maybe he's gone off trying to find you."

"Nonsense," I said. But when Socksie showed up the day I came home, Connie cited that as proof. He had lost an immense amount of weight, which we accounted for by the fact that he had been away from the house ten days, and he lay quietly beside me on the couch for another week or so while I recovered from my back operation, which also did not signal us that he was ill because he loved a body to press up against. Then the first afternoon I was up and around he disappeared again.

Walking slowly the next morning, I looked for him along the riverbank, then circled and came back along the perennial border, past the middle garden, and on through the wisteria arch. There, lying on

his side in the shade under the yew tree, was Socksie.
A fly was crawling on his closed eye. He had come
out to the garden to die, being as little trouble to us
in death as he had been in life, staying close when he
could but going off to deal with his illness alone. I
wished he had somehow let us know he was dying.
I wished he had come to us to be held at the end, but
I was touched by his bravery. I hope, if it plays out
that way, I can mimic his ungrudging acceptance of
the inevitable.

As I have learned much about living from cats, I
have also learned something about dying: the natu-
ralness of aging and death most of all, but, too, the
way the manner of death matches the personality.
Strong-minded Kate fought back to the end. Gentle
Socksie resigned himself and drifted away. Bitty, I
imagine, went gaily off, adventuring and bested in
battle by a creature better armed than he.

And Chester? I don't know how to think about
Chessie. Or perhaps it is that I do not like to think
about his death at all because Connie and I were
responsible for it. I was home alone late on a summer's day when I heard snarling screams coming
from in front of the house, screams of a sort I had
heard once before when I observed two raccoons
fighting. A friend of ours had, the week before, been
attacked in her garden by a rabid raccoon, and there
had been warnings in the newspapers and on the
radio about not approaching any raccoon abroad in

daylight because these nocturnal animals do not let themselves be seen unless the illness of rabies has destroyed their caution. Thus, I raced to the front porch but halted on the top step.

The raccoon, a large one, was crouched in the driveway. It snarled again and lunged under my car. Horrified, I saw that it had caught Chester by the hind leg and was dragging him out. I snatched up a flowerpot and loosed it like a boomerang. It landed beside the raccoon, broke, and the pieces flew in every direction. The raccoon, startled, let Chessie go and turned to look at me. I slung a second pot, and when it too shattered, spraying shards and dirt, the raccoon snarled in frustration, turned, and swaying like an elephant, made its way slowly to the bridge. Midway across, it looked back, screamed again, then continued on and disappeared into the woods on the other side of the river.

I ran to get Chessie and carried him inside. His back legs were soaked with blood and the raccoon's saliva. I held them under running water, washing them off as best I could, but because of his long hair and the general mess, I could not tell the extent of damage. I wrapped him in a towel and held him while I dialed our vet. It was after hours and all I got was a message that, in case of emergency, a clinic four towns away was open twenty-four hours a day.

It was a forty-five-minute drive, and another forty-five minutes went by before a vet was available. The doctor shaved Chessie's legs, revealing a number of punctures and gashes, one requiring stitches. "I have to report this to the state," the doctor said, "and because of the danger of rabies, the cat will either have to be put down or kept in isolation in a cage for six months."

"Even if he has been vaccinated against rabies?"

"Perhaps not, if it's a recent enough vaccination, I'm not sure."

The vaccination was not recent. Our own vet's records showed that it had been three years before and Chessie was overdue for a booster shot. The vet confirmed that he would have to be quarantined for six months. We would have done that, and knowing Chessie so well, we were sure we would immediately spot any signs that he was developing rabies and could take immediate steps to protect ourselves. But . . . But Connie and I were leaving in two days on a long-planned trip to Europe, and for the three weeks we would be gone, a friend was going to be staying in the house. He did not know Chester; he had never had cats of his own; he was not likely to recognize unusual behavior; he was doing us a favor by taking care of the animals and house. Could we risk exposing him to rabies? We decided not.

To this day, Connie and I cannot bear to speak of the decision. We both intuited that Chessie was all right, that he would not come down with rabies, that we were killing a strong, sweet, dignified, elegant creature with years yet to go. Did we do the right thing? Could we, should we, have done something else?

I remember a long-ago conversation with the most coolly rational person of my acquaintance who spoke of visiting an uncle with a painful and disfiguring illness in a Swiss clinic. He had waited and waited for her to come, counting on her to help him end his life. She utterly sympathized with his decision but found that she could not bring him the pills he begged her for. I would have, I thought then, but after Chessie, I am not so sure. I do not believe death is an evil. I believe it is sometimes a great good, and I believe people have a right to decide when life has become intolerable for them. But I understand now how very, very difficult it is to be the onlooker who says: Yes, end this life.

It is easier to be the one who is leaving life. I once had two operations ten days apart, and after the second, I hallucinated sliding, sliding, down an infinite, treeless, mud-covered slope. With no strength to cling and nothing to cling to, I was sliding off the edge of the world. *Ah*, I though, *I am dying. How easy. How simple.* I had no objection. It did not matter in the least to me.

After four days I turned a corner and started back into life, but what was strange and frightening to me in the recovery weeks that followed was my indifference. People I cared about, work I cared about, interests that had absorbed me, concerns that

had worried me—they had no meaning for me; my
investment in them was gone. I lay hour after hour
on a deck overlooking the ocean, and life to me was
as featureless as the sea I gazed at.

One day a gull drifted into sight. Its wings still,
it rested on the air currents and floated, will-less,
this way and that, wherever the breeze carried it.
Time went by and still it drifted without volition,
out to sea, back toward land, high in the sky, down
near the water. Finally, as the sun was going down,
the gull turned toward land, set its course, and
began to beat its wings, slowly at first, then with
more and more purpose. Now it had a destination
and it was working to get there.

I am like that gull, I thought. *I am drifting now. But
purpose will come back, I will begin to make an effort, and
everything will take on meaning again.*

After that, I understood that life has no intrinsic
meaning, only the meaning one gives to it. And the
meaning one brings to life greatly influences what
one gets out of it, which is why it is important to
learn everything one can about the art of living.

The art can be learned from great lives, from
thoughtful people, from books, from talk, from
nature, from stories—even from cats—if one gathers
in the truths that lie all around and makes them
one's own.

Seven lessons from seven cats: From Poppy, to
know oneself. From Chester, to accept oneself. From
Socksie, to govern oneself. From Trot, to value one-

self. From Sweet William, to stay in touch with oneself. From Kate, to be oneself. And from Bitty, to go out from oneself in love and kindness.

Sometimes there will be failures, your own and other people's. When they come, turn again to the cat. Very little in this life is more consoling than a purring body in one's lap and the soft feel of fur under one's hand.